IRELAND
Past and Present

Endpapers
Haymaking in County Donegal.

Half title page
Children in the Georgian doorways of Dublin.

Title page
A stream on the remote and beautiful Dingle Peninsula, County Kerry.

Contents page
Dry stone walls in the fields of County Kerry.

Published in Ireland by
Gill and Macmillan Ltd
Goldenbridge
Dublin 8
with associated companies in
Auckland, Delhi, Gaborone, Hamburg, Harare,
Hong Kong, Johannesburg, Kuala Lumpur, Lagos, London,
Manzini, Melbourne, Mexico City, Nairobi,
New York, Singapore, Tokyo

Editor Anne Cope
Design Megra Mitchell
Picture research Sheila Corr
Production Hugh Allan

0 7171 1966 1

Published in the United Kingdom by PRION,
an imprint of Multimedia Books Limited,
32-34 Gordon House Road, London NW5 1LP

Typeset by Wyvern Typesetting, Bristol, England
Printed in Italy by Poligrafici Calderara SpA, Bologna

IRELAND
Past and Present

Brendan Kennelly

Terence Brown
David Hanly
Sean Kilfeather
Brendán O hEithir
Liam de Paor
Sean White

Gill and Macmillan

Contents

Foreword

Brendan Kennelly

Ireland is a small, pleasant, gossipy, passionate country whose history can at times become mythology and whose mythological figures and events are sometimes treated as if they were historical facts. That history, long and troubled, shows that the Irish are a race of shrewd, resourceful survivors. The mythology, rich and ancient, demonstrates the co-existence in Irish culture and society of the heroic and the squalid, the magnanimous and the opportunistic. It all adds up to the complex identity of one of the most fascinating little countries in the world.

This book takes a keen look at crucial aspects of that identity. The simple words "Northern Ireland" will conjure up a look of sadness and horrified disbelief on the faces of many people throughout the civilized world, and will prompt them to ask: "How civilized is that particular part of the so-called civilized world?" Ulster is a relatively small province in which tit-for-tat murders by Protestants of Catholics, by Catholics of Protestants, are commonplace. Why? And why has such an appalling state of affairs continued for over 20 years now? Is there any hope of even a glimpse of a resolution of the problem? Or is Ireland a country where horror goes on forever while politicians make vain efforts to "get around a table" in an attempt to talk to each other?

This entrapment in almost daily atrocity seems all the more incredible when one considers that Southern Ireland, the Republic, is quickly adjusting to its status as a lively, progressive part of the New Europe. Ireland, the traditional land of saints and scholars, is fast becoming a country of yuppies and dynamic young businessmen and businesswomen determined to make their profitable mark on the commercial life of the Continent. There's a strong, vital sense of connection between the new young educated Irish and their European counterparts. The image of the traditional Paddy, bull-necked and drunk in London or Liverpool, has almost completely disappeared. Ireland is opening up in a consciously materialistic, trained and efficient manner to the teeming challenges and opportunities of the final decade of the twentieth century.

Yet many of the old pains and problems are still there. The Northern "troubles," unemployment, emigration, a rising crime rate, poverty, especially in Dublin and in other cities to a lesser extent, a depressed countryside—all these co-exist with the sense that Ireland is achieving a new European identity. The problems are many and real; and though these problems are profound and pervasive there is also emerging a new, well-educated and ambitious generation of young men and women capable of dealing with them in efficient modern ways. Ireland today is an extremely complex place; whole-hearted and strong-minded attempts to analyse and describe the origins, nature and likely consequences of that complexity are made in this book. The reader will get a vivid sense of the development of Ireland from an ancient society to a busy modern country.

Religion is dealt with. So is sport. It can hardly be argued that there's much sport in Irish religion, either of the Catholic or Protestant denomination. But few people will deny that sport achieves a religious fervor and intensity in almost all parts of our green, pleasant, gossipy, hospitable and murderous land.

Political and social analysts agree that Ireland is undergoing deep and far-reaching changes just now. Some of these changes are perhaps so subtle as to be almost impossible to analyse accurately. But other changes that affect traditional values and ways of life which seem to have altered little since the nineteenth century are now running through the life of the country. Those changes are exciting to contemplate because they affect rich and poor, young and old, men and women. Women especially, perhaps. Or is it a law of nature that when women's lives are drastically altered men's lives also undergo deep and resonant changes, however reluctantly? The new, young, independent women of Ireland are startling and impressive people.

Is it any wonder that such a small country has produced so many major writers, and continues to do so? Ireland is a furiously articulate island, brilliant, cynical, bitterly critical of its writers, almost as critical in fact as many of the writers are of each other. Dr. Samuel Johnson, who, I feel, would have felt very much at home in an Irish pub, put the matter most succinctly: "The Irish are not in a conspiracy to cheat the world by false representations of the merits of their countrymen. No, sir; the Irish are a fair people—they never speak well of one another."

In this book, the Irish speak and write of each other. They do so as truthfully and candidly as they can. That's why the book is sharp, informative, funny, sad, maddening and enjoyable. Like Ireland itself, you might say.

Brendan Kennelly

Above *A cottage window at Ballymascanlon, County Louth.*

Left *Lough Leane, County Kerry, one of many beauty spots around Killarney and the Ring of Kerry in southwest Ireland.*

The valley below Glenariff, County Antrim, with the sea in the distance.

Left *A colorful quilt hanging over a fence to dry.*

Above *Children playing in a street in Belfast, Northern Ireland.*

Below *Modern sculpture in Parnell Square, Dublin.*

Left *Seagulls squabble over scraps from fishing boats at Killybegs, County Donegal.*

Left *The brooding beauty of Beara Peninsula, County Cork.*

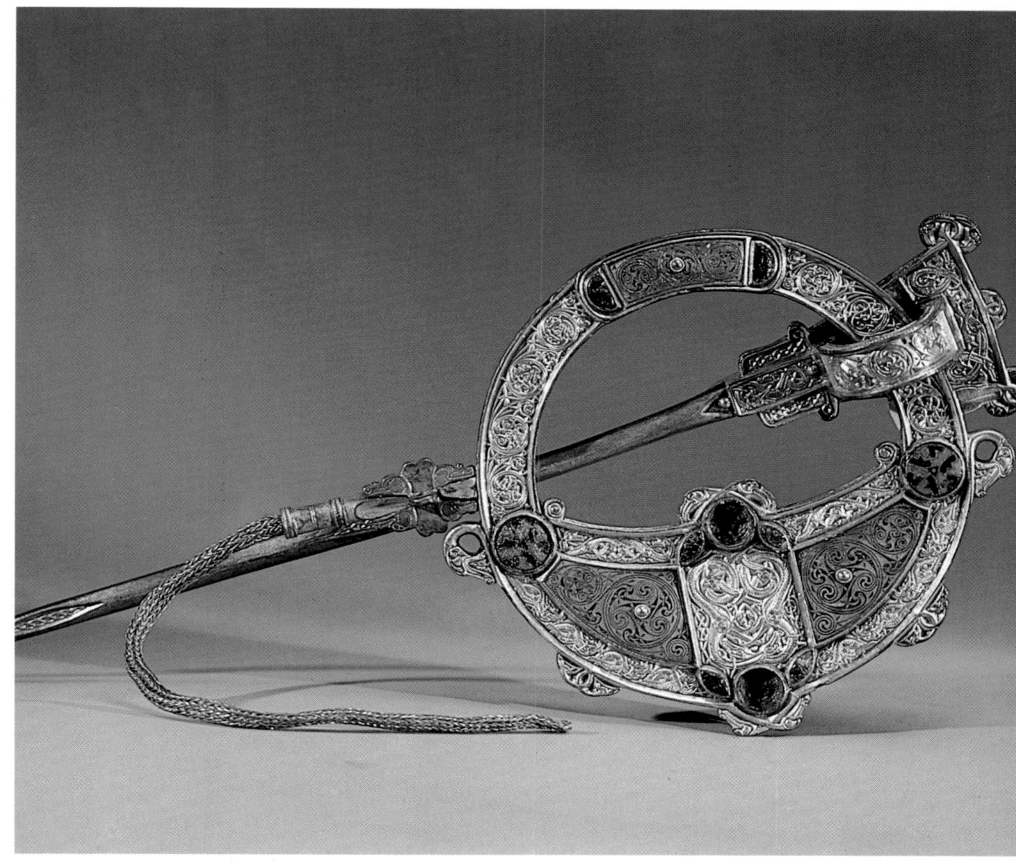

Above *The Tara brooch, a beautiful eighth-century ornament of cast silver gilt. (National Museum of Ireland, Dublin)*

Slate has replaced the original thatch on the roof of this cottage in the west of Ireland.

Aran sweaters, hand-knitted in traditional patterns, evolved to combat the uncertain weather of Ireland's Atlantic coast. The Aran Islands lie in Galway Bay, 30 miles from the mainland.

Tory Island
Giant's Causeway
Lough Foyle
Foyle
Derry
DERRY
Bann
ANTRIM
DONEGAL
Carrickfergus
ATLANTIC OCEAN
Killybegs
Lough Neagh
Belfast
TYRONE
Lagan
Lough Erne
Dromore
ULSTER
Ben Bulben
Enniskillen
Armagh
DOWN
LEITRIM
Dundrum
FERMANAGH
ARMAGH
Sligo
MONAGHAN
SLIGO
CONNACHT
Achill Island
CAVAN
LOUTH
MAYO
New Grange
Monasterboice
Mellifont
Croagh Patrick
ROSCOMMON
LONGFORD
Drogheda
Kells
MEATH
Tara
DUBLIN
Trim
Clifden
Boyne
GALWAY
Athlone
WESTMEATH
Dunboyne
Maynooth
Dublin
Galway
Clonmacnoise
LEINSTER
Clonfert
OFFALY
Liffey
Galway Bay
Shannon
KILDARE
Aran Islands
WICKLOW
Lisdoonvarna
Glendalough
Lough Derg
LAOIS
CLARE
Durrow
Quin
IRISH SEA
TIPPERARY
KILKENNY
CARLOW
Limerick
Kilkenny
Suir
LIMERICK
Enniscorthy
Cashel
Listowel
Jerpoint Abbey
WEXFORD
MUNSTER
Clonmel
Wexford
Tintern Abbey
Dingle Peninsula
Gallarus Oratory
Dingle
KERRY
Doneraile
Waterford
WATERFORD
Blackwater
Killarney
Slea Head
The Paps
Lough Leane
Blarney
Cork
Lee
CORK
The Skelligs
Bantry
Bantry Bay

Right *The basalt columns of the Giant's Causeway stride into the sea off the northeast coast of Ireland. According to legend, the causeway was built by Fionn MacCumhail so that his lady love, a giantess who lived on the Scottish island of Staffa, could visit him without getting her feet wet. True enough, the causeway runs across the North Channel to Rathlin, Islay, Staffa and Mull.*

Ancient Ireland 1

David Hanly

Let us dip firstly—and briefly—into Ireland's prehistory. The first people to arrive in Ireland came from Scandinavia to Britain, then moved across the narrow strait between Northern Ireland and Scotland and spread out to Lough Neagh, to Roscommon, to Carlow and to Limerick.

They came around 6000 BC, and we know little about these Middle Stone Age or Mesolithic people. We know nothing about their houses or their graves, and the tools they left were the most primitive flint instruments, found in garbage dumps on the edges of swamps from which they got their food. At that time, except for its lakes and rivers Ireland was covered by dense woodland.

By the year 3000 BC the first farmers had arrived. These Neolithic people were almost entirely self-sufficient: they were hunters, potters, even axe-manufacturers, mass-producing and exporting axes over 5000 years ago. They had elaborate religious rituals and raised enormous burial monuments for their dead—megalithic tombs and passage graves, the stones elaborately decorated with spirals, zig-zags and whorls.

About the year 2000 BC, following a further great technological advance in the Middle East, the first prospectors and metal-workers reached the island, ushering in the Bronze Age, leaving behind pottery vessels finely crafted and exquisitely decorated.

By the year 600 BC the production of iron had advanced on the Continent, and several tribes, skilled in the production and deployment of iron, were establishing themselves in Europe. These peoples—led by rich and powerful chiefs—spoke the same language, Celtic, the forerunner of the Irish spoken in Ireland today. The Greeks knew them as the *Keltoi*, or Celts.

The Celts stretched through the heartland of Europe, from Bohemia to Austria and southern Germany, Switzerland and the eastern borders of France. This confederation of tribes—linked by language, religion and culture—emerged as the first civilization north of the Alps. At the height of their influence (just before 300 BC) they stretched from Finisterre to the Black Sea, and from the North Sea to the Mediterranean. They lacked cohesion and never forged even a state, let alone an empire, nor did they ever achieve ethnic unity.

But over seven centuries of cultural dominance they most certainly laid the economic, social and artistic foundations of Northern European civilization. They invented chain armor, introduced the Greeks and Romans to soap, and were the first to put shoes on horses. They were the first to use the iron plowshare and the rotary flour mill, and they pioneered

Above *Newgrange, a passage grave overlooking the Boyne river valley in County Meath, is one of Europe's most impressive prehistoric monuments, dating from 2500 BC. The Gaels regarded the site as an Otherworld divine dwelling. This view shows one of the two stone basins inside the grave.*

women's rights thousands of years before feminists found a pulpit.

But their real passion was war. In war the Celts would strut arrogantly before the enemy, their hair stiffened with lime, brandishing their arms, boasting their prowess, bellowing scorn and abuse. Diodorus Siculus, the Greek historian, tells us they beheaded their victims and tied the heads to the necks of their horses. "They embalm in cedar oil the heads of the most distinguished enemies and preserve them carefully in a chest and display them with pride to strangers."

"The whole race," wrote the Greek geographer Strabo, "is madly fond of war."

The whole race was also madly fond of eating and drinking. When they weren't fighting, hunting, wrestling or chariot-racing, they would gather in a chieftain's house, sprawl on their animal furs and "drink and eat themselves into a stupor or a state of madness," according to Diodorus.

By 150 BC the Celts were well established in all parts of Ireland, and in establishing themselves—deliberately or by attrition—they wiped out almost all traces of the peoples who preceded them. The culture and traditions of the Mesolithic hunters and the Neolithic farmers, of the Bronze Age metal workers and of the herdsmen, all faded. By the time Irish history properly begins—in the fifth century AD—all of the people of Ireland were utterly Celticized, sharing a common Celtic culture and a common language; they were the Gaels and Gaelic was their language. They were fey, ribald and superstitious, they enjoyed fighting and took palpable pleasure from melancholy, and their powerful imagination had already fashioned and fine-detailed one of the most richly varied mythologies of Europe.

It would be foolhardy to attempt to pinpoint when the great Irish myths and sagas evolved. That would be an impossible task; the stories had their genesis in the impermeable mists of Irish prehistory and developed through centuries of oral rendition, naturally resulting in distortion, accretion, duplication and even contradiction.

The Celts loved a story. *The Voyage of Bran* tells how an Ulster king was told a story by his *file*, or poet, every winter night from Samhain (Halloween) to Beltene, or the first day of May. It is possible that the *fili* memorized entire tales, but it is more likely that they knew the outlines and extemporized the minutiae, although later graduates of the Bardic schools were expected to master literally hundreds of classical stories.

It was not until the seventh, eighth and following centuries AD that learned Irishmen—mostly monks—began to transcribe the great stories, a mutation that also caused disfigurement and historical corruption. It is true that nothing connected with the Irish myths and sagas is "incontrovertible," in any proper sense, but it is equally true that there was an underlying determination on the part of the scribes to fashion for Ireland a history on the models of the Bible and of Greece and Rome, what historian John MacNeill called "synthetic Irish history." These men in their spartan monasteries spent hour after cramp-inducing hour transmuting the oral to the written, leaving Ireland a legacy lost to almost every other Celtic group.

So what are these great tales? What was it about these stories that made them worthy of transcription a thousand years ago and still makes them worthy of publication as we approach the end of the second millennium AD?

Tradition and convention have ordained that the stories be divided into four cycles: *The*

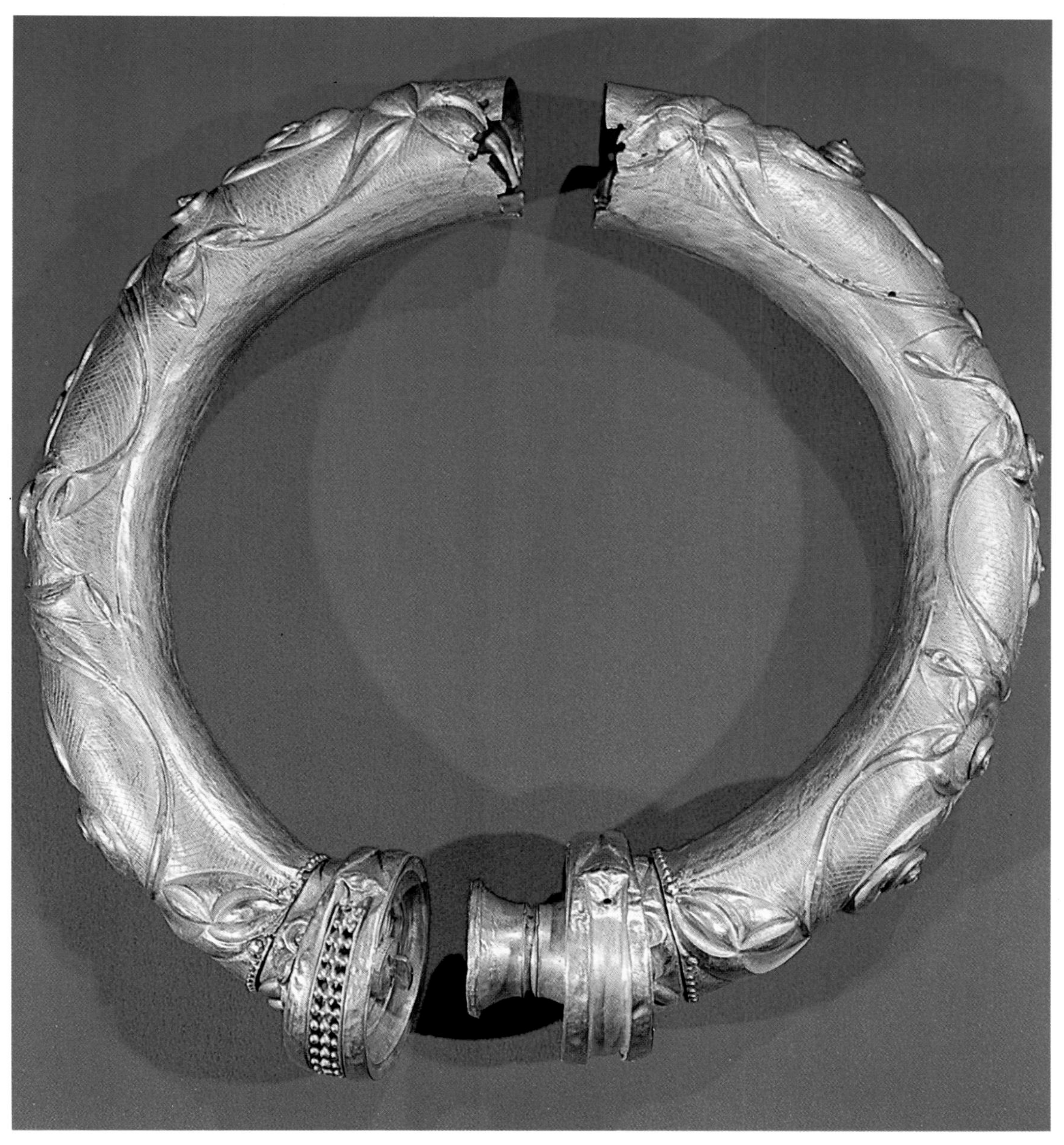

Far left *To the Gaels, the Hill of Tara (High Place of Kings) in County Meath was sacred. Feis Temhra, a ritual marriage feast confirming the status of each new king, was held here until the sixth century AD. Many Irish myths and legends attach to these ancient earthworks.*

Left *This exquisite gold neck ornament, known as the Broighter Collar, was made in the first century AD. It was found in County Derry and is now in the National Museum of Ireland in Dublin.*

Mythological Cycle, whose stories are set mainly around Tara and the burial mounds of the Boyne Valley; *The Ulster Cycle*, also known as the *Cuchulainn Cycle*, wherein we meet the paradigm of Irish heroes, and which details the allegedly historical events in Ulster some centuries before or after the birth of Christ; *The Kings Cycle*, which concentrates on the (again purportedly historical) kings; and *The Fenian* or *Ossianic Cycle*, concerning Fionn MacCumhail and his adventures with his band of roving warriors.

While these groupings are convenient, it should be remembered that the manuscripts themselves do not justify such cycles, nor is there any chronological justification for them—they are modern and artificial, but, as we have said, they are convenient.

For our knowledge of the earliest mythology we are indebted to the twelfth-century *Leabhar Gabhala Eireann*, or the *Book of Invasions*, which describes six invasions of the island. The first of these happened before the Deluge and was led by Banbha, also one of the earliest names for Ireland. Next came Partholawn, who fought the first battle ever in Ireland against the demonic Fomhorians. Partholawn cleared four plains, built the first guest house, brewed the first beer (Oh, wise Partholawn!) and established legal suretyship, and for all of these good things he and his people perished in a plague.

Next to arrive were the even more hapless followers of Nemhedh, who were under the thumb of the Fomhorians and were eventually driven out, but not before more plains were created and the island had become a geographical entity, with "local habitation and a name."

The Fir Bolg followed, dividing the country into five provinces—Ulster, Leinster, Munster, Connacht and Meath. They also introduced the notion of kingship, before the next invasion by the Tuatha De Danann (the People of the Goddess Dana). These people fought and triumphed over the Fir Bolg at the first Battle of Moytura, but were then forced into epic conflict with the ancient enemy, the terrible Fomhorians.

The Second Battle of Moytura is mythologi-

Left *A cottage nestles among the ancient stone walls of Dun Conor, a fort on the Aran Islands.*

cally the most important of all the stories in the *Book of Invasions*. The Tuatha De Danann—a pre-Christian pantheon of Gods—confronted and utterly vanquished the evil and demonic Fomhorians (literally "under-demons"). The manner of their triumph and the personalities of the deities are perfect manifestations of the pagan Irish gods and their feats. (And, incidentally, of their nature, for they are not, like their Greek counterparts, awesomely dreadful, brutal and unforgiving. As Aodh de Blacam has remarked, in the literature they are "mighty but friendly beings who share with mankind the adventure of life.")

Among the old Irish gods were Dana, the ever-fertile mother goddess; Dagda the droll, with his mighty club and bottomless cauldron, a kind of Celtic Jupiter; Angus, his son, the god of youth and love; Dian Ceacht, the god of healing; Goibniu, the gods' artificer; and Lugh of the Long Arm, under whose direction the others crafted mighty weapons, lifted and hurled the Irish mountains, hid the lakes and rivers, and cast showers of fire.

Not all of the stories in the *Book of Invasions* are as monstrously bloody as *The Second Battle of Moytura*, but they are all imbued with the same wondrous mixture of the magical, the supernatural and the fantastic, where exaggeration is the norm and where people and events bear tenuous (or no) links with reality.

It is well to remember that all the stories in

Below *The Ardagh Chalice was found during potato digging in 1867 near Ardagh, County Limerick. It now resides in the National Museum of Ireland in Dublin.*

Left *The Paps of Anu in County Kerry are named after the goddess Anu or Dana, mother of the gods. An earth and fertility goddess, Dana was especially associated with the province of Munster.*

the *Book of Invasions* lead up to the arrival in Ireland of the Sons of Mil, the Milesians, who defeated the Tuatha De Danann and whose descendants, the Gaels, were ever afterwards the dominant people of Ireland. It was the Gaels who composed the narrative and on them fell the responsibility for imposing on it a continuity, an evolution, a binding of the different races into a nation. This they did and well, but with one remarkable omission—the Celts left no myth of the creation of the world or, if they did, it was gently expunged by Christian literati who were not unprejudiced in these matters and wished the history of Ireland to be not totally out of line with the Bible and various historians such as Eusebius and Orosius, whose views were distinctly Christian.

So it was the Gaels who composed *The Second Battle of Moytura*, and also another story in the *Book of Invasions*, *The Wooing of Etain*. This relates how the lovely Etain is wooed and won by Midir in the Otherworld, changed into a fly by her rival Fuamnach and blown into this world, where she is thrice reborn before being wooed back again into the Otherworld by Midir.

This Celtic Otherworld is not the silent, gloomy, classical underworld, peopled by shades, pale, mute and sullen. On the contrary it is Elysian, a place of innocent love, of beautiful women, of enchanted music. It is sometimes under the ground, sometimes under the sea, sometimes far across the sea; it is the land of the perpetually young, the land of the immortal, the land of the women; it is the land of tranquillity and peace. And yet, with the inevitable paradox, its inhabitants fight each other and on occasion—a recurring motif throughout the history of Irish literature—have their feuds resolved by a human, as when Cuchulainn is called upon to help Labhraidh of the Swift Sword-hand, to be rewarded with the love of the beautiful Fann.

Cuchulainn is the great hero of Ulster, the man in the gap against the loathed Connachtaigh, and the protagonist of the *Táin Bó Cuailgne* (*The Cattle Raid of Cooley*), the magnificent central saga of *The Ulster Cycle*. This cycle has as much violence as the previous one, but it is more logically rooted. Although the feats are as outrageously exaggerated, the hero (while seemingly omnicompetent) is nevertheless vulnerable, a sort of Celtic Achilles. The story of the *Táin* is the story of a row about cattle, a universal saga and one that continues to this day.

Queen Maeve of Connacht covets the Brown Bull of Cooley in Ulster so that she may have a bull as powerful as her husband's. Ulster is not lightly attacked by her enemies—nor is she still—but suddenly the Ulster warriors are struck down by an illness which makes them as "weak and helpless as a woman in child-birth." All, that is, except Setanta, or Cuchulainn (the Hound of Culainn) as he has since been renamed.

He defends Ulster with magnificent energy and valor, even (and finally) against his foster-brother and best friend, Ferdia, who crossed over to the side of the Connachtaigh and was cajoled by Maeve into confronting Cuchulainn. But what chance had Ferdia against a warrior in the terrible grip of the *riastradh*, or battle frenzy? The description of this battle frenzy leaves little wonder that once, at the sight of Cuchulainn's frenzy, one hundred of Maeve's warriors fell dead from horror. Still, he was finally defeated and took his last breath having tied himself to a pillar-stone so that he might die standing rather than lying down.

Thus departed Cuchulainn, greatest of the Red Branch knights, mightiest of the mighty, the quintessential Irish mythical hero: barbaric, poetical, full of boastful rant, proud, fearless and contradictory, vulnerable to grief, and choosing one brief hour of immortalizing glory rather than an eternity of tedious worthiness.

Other stories in the *Cycle* are hard put to match the wild, aristocratic grandeur of the *Táin*, but they are nonetheless splendid for that. For instance, the chief of the preliminary stories to the *Táin*, Deirdre and the Sons of Usna, is pure romantic tragedy and moves towards its resolution with the inexorable logic of the tragedies of Shakespeare or Sophocles.

It tells how Deirdre's fatal beauty was coveted by the aged King Conor, and how she fell in love with Naoise, the son of Usna, and eloped with him to Scotland, together with his brothers Ainle and Ardan. But they were enticed back to Ireland and brought to their doom partly because of Naoise's masculine contempt for a woman's intuition. When Conor broke his oath and had the three sons of Usna beheaded, he took Deirdre by force. One day, out on the

Far left *This bronze statue of the dying hero Cuchulainn stands inside the General Post Office in Dublin, where the Republic of Ireland was declared in 1916.*

Left *The steep cliffs of Benbulben in County Sligo. In Gaelic mythology, this is where Diarmuid was slain by the magic boar who had once been his foster-brother. The poet W.B. Yeats is buried in the graveyard at Drumcliff nearby.*

Right *The River Shannon as it flows through Athlone, County Westmeath, in the heart of Ireland. Athlone was named after Ath Luain, the Brown Bull of Cooley, whom Queen Maeve pursued across the river in her invasion of Ulster in the Táin Bó Cuailgne .*

chariot with Deirdre and Owen of Duracht, Conor said: "Deirdre, what is it that you hate most of all on earth?" And she replied, "Thou thyself and Owen of Duracht." And Conor said, "Deirdre, the glance of thee between me and Owen is like the glance of a ewe between rams." And Deirdre threw herself headfirst from the chariot, smashed her skull against a rock and died—and in her life and death inspired more Irish writing than any other mythical female, from Yeats and James Stephens to Synge and Lady Gregory.

The centerpiece of *The Ulster Cycle* is the great Emhain Macha, seat of the Ulster kings, near present-day Armagh. The Red Branch knights were taught their skills inside its trenches and ramparts, great feasts were held within its walls, and it was there, during the long winter nights, that the *fili* recited the epic narratives, fashioned and shaped by generation after generation of their successors, into the legends that survive today.

The *fili* were powerful. Their power rested in their ability with words, particularly satirical words. These struck mortal fear into the hearts of the most powerful of men, even kings, who were the solid fountainheads of the social order. The king stories, while they are imbued with all the heroism of *The Ulster Cycle*, nevertheless have a different emphasis: they are concerned more with the status and function of kingship than with heroic values and ideals.

The great Cormac MacAirt, who died in AD 266, is the prime exemplar of the kingly gifts. That a king should be valorous, energetic and of sublime sensibility goes without saying, but such virtues would not mark him off from a thousand knights. He must also deliver, and

Above *More than 300 ogham stones survive in Ireland, mostly in the southern counties. This one is at Kilmalkedar in County Kerry. Ogham script, the earliest form of written Irish, was a secret writing derived from Latin and used for inscriptions cut into the edges of stones.*

Left *Achill Head, County Mayo, epitomizes the wild west coast of Ireland.*

be seen to deliver, judgements of unquestionable disinterestedness. When Conaire Mor—a compassionate king whose reign ushered in tranquillity and prosperity—exhibited a more-than-just share of mercy when dealing with his foster-brothers, he sparks off a reaction that moves him ineluctably to his own death in a welter of violence, as we learn in the tragic story of *The Destruction of the Hostel of Da Derga*. Quite a different emphasis is to be found in *Ronan's Killing of His Own Kin*. When Maol Fhothartaigh, son of Ronan, King of Leinster, spurns the advances of his father's young wife, she destroys him with her jealous anger.

The king stories show a distinct de-emphasizing of the hero as a hero and personality, but underline the status of the hero as a king whose heroism manifests itself not so much in the triumphs of combat, but in the exercise of social responsibility and in the recognition of kingship as the paramount institution in Irish society, to be fought for, achieved and lived up to.

In *The Fenian* or *Ossianic Cycle* we are back once more in the spirit of the wilderness with

Right *The dolmen at Haroldstown, County Carlow, is a portal dolmen. Once covered by earth and used as a burial chamber, it consists of upright stones and a single capstone. Every dolmen in Ireland is known as 'Diarmuid and Grainne's Bed,' an allusion to the tale of Grainne's elopement with Diarmuid and their flight from the vengeance of Fionn.*

Fionn MacCumhail and the Fianna, a band of professional warriors without tribal loyalty, rootless and mobile, yet recognized as serving a valid function; they defend Ireland against its enemies, whether from within or without or from the Otherworld. They roam the length and breadth of the island, hunting, fishing, fighting, falling in love, continuously communing with and marveling at every aspect of nature.

Over the centuries *The Ossianic Cycle* displaced *The Ulster Cycle* in popularity, and Fionn and Oisin and Diarmuid and Grainne became known universally as Cuchulainn never did. Perhaps it was because of the great love story of Diarmuid and Grainne (every dolmen in Ireland is known as "Diarmuid and Grainne's Bed"), which is analogous to the romance of Tristan and Iseult; perhaps because the feats of Fionn and his warriors are not so wildly improbable and therefore more sympathetic to the contemporary mind; or perhaps because of the constant and lyric evocation of their love for nature.

Whatever the reason, or combination of reasons, the *Ossianic* tales swept Europe in the eighteenth century and permeated European

Below *Many examples of early Irish stonework can be found on White Island and Devenish Island on the shores of Lough Erne, County Fermanagh. On the far wall in this picture are a human mask and eight figures. One of the figures is an abbot and the others are probably warriors.*

Above *Croagh Patrick (Patrick's Mountain) on the Atlantic coast of County Mayo is where St. Patrick prayed and fasted during Lent in AD 441. The pilgrimage that takes place here in July each year evolved from the pagan festival of Lughnasa, marking the end of summer.*

art and life in a way that the Irish vernacular tradition was not to do again for almost 200 years. A Scotsman named James MacPherson based his poems *Fingal* and *Temora* on *The Ossianic Cycle*. MacPherson claimed they were written by Ossian (Oisin) and found and translated by himself.

It was a magnificent fraud, but it fooled the Edinburgh literati (except for David Hume) and, for a while, their London counterparts. And it bowled over the Europeans. Goethe compared Ossian to Shakespeare. Napoleon read the poems and his marshal, Bernadotte, took them to Sweden and gave the name Oscar to successive Swedish kings (and, would you believe, gave the names Oscar *and* Fingal to the son of the court physician, Dr. Wilde).

Meanwhile, Ossian's genius pervaded European art. Ossianic themes were painted by Angelica Kauffmann and Abilgard the Dane. The French painters Gérard, Girodet and Ingres painted massive pictures which mixed the Fianna warriors and Napoleon's soldiers, and those pictures hung in the imperial apartments in Paris and Rome.

One of the outstanding stories in *The Ossianic Cycle* is the *Colloquy of the Ancients*, in which the last great pagan heroes of the Fianna, Oisin and Caoilte, converse at length with Ireland's first Christian bishop, St. Patrick. The "tonsured one" had at last arrived and with him the myths and sagas knit themselves into the true history of Ireland.

Patrick arrived in Ireland in the middle of the fifth century and was the author of the earliest documents known to have been written on the island. It is with him that Irish history really begins. In his own words, he "baptized thousands, ordained clerics everywhere, gave presents to kings, was put in irons, lived in daily expectation of murder, treachery and captivity, journeyed everywhere in many dangers, and rejoiced to see the flock of the Lord in Ireland growing splendidly with the greatest care and the sons and daughters of kings becoming monks and virgins of Christ."

The conversion to Christianity was rapid. Patrick set up an episcopal system of Church government, but he also, more importantly, introduced the monastic life to the island and was gratified by the large numbers of new converts who embraced it. Within two centuries of his death Ireland had become unique in Western Christendom in having its most important churches ruled by a monastic hierarchy. Monasteries were sited all over the island and constituted the earliest settlements. They were nothing like the later great monasteries. Life was austere, rules were strict, and the life of each monk was a continuing act of self-denial.

In the monasteries the copying of manuscripts was an important occupation. The élite among the monks were the scribes; the libraries and scriptoria had manuscripts suspended in satchels by leather straps from the walls, and an ample supply of writing materials—waxed tablets, parchment, quills and inkhorns.

And in these monasteries the great myths of the Gaels were written down for the first time. Not all of them have survived the centuries—some were lost and some were hidden, never to be found. Others were destroyed in the flames that engulfed the monasteries when they were attacked by the Irish. And others were burnt by the marauders of the seventh invasion of Ireland, the Vikings.

Below *The monks of the early Irish Church communed with God in very lonely places. These are the Skellig Islands off the southwest coast of County Kerry, raided by the Vikings and finally abandoned in the thirteenth century.*

Right *The monastery of Clonmacnoise, built on a windswept plain in a bend in the River Shannon, was founded by St. Ciaran in the sixth century. For many centuries it could only be reached by boat or by a raised ramp known as the Pilgrims' Causeway.*

Vikings and Normans 2

Sean White

The country that the Vikings began to invade from the seventh century onwards, and that the Normans invaded in the twelfth century, was quiet and green, an island on the edge of the world. It had escaped the invasions of the Romans and barbarians; indeed the customs and way of life of its Celtic inhabitants had hardly changed in the previous thousand years.

At that time Ireland contained at least a hundred small kingdoms, made up of closely related families living within the protection of earthen ring forts in wattle houses thatched in straw, rearing crops and tending cattle. Towns or great centers of power and trade did not exist. The kingdoms made treaties, healed quarrels, traded with foreign merchants and held singing and poetry contests at seasonal fairs and festivals. They fought over cattle or women, rarely over territory.

Art was literary rather than graphic. The *file* was a wise man and privileged, whose function it was to preserve tradition and the genealogies of the royal and noble families, and to expound and record the law. The *fili* presided at the inauguration of kings. They wrote poems to praise or condemn; they had the power of words. Instead of the free creative inspiration of the modern poet, the *fili* claimed a traditional semi-magical authority which may have descended to them from the ancient Druids.

The one intrusion into the seamless pattern of Irish life was the coming of Christianity. Far from uniting Ireland with the rest of Europe, this produced that singularly isolated and very peculiar organization, the early Irish Church.

The Christian church that St. Patrick founded in the fifth century showed, in its simpler forms, the complex legal structures that the church had borrowed from the Roman Empire. The saint set up a territorial episcopate, a structure of church discipline with canon law controlling such important matters as clerical celibacy, marriage rules and the independent property rights of the church.

Monks and monasteries were all under proper ecclesiastical authority even if they had some exotic hermetic practices borrowed from Egypt. In the centuries between the Viking raids and the Norman invasion, the Irish Church developed and continued to practice its own peculiar forms. Instead of bishops there were abbots, many of them laymen, ruling the church. An hereditary clergy evolved which held the many monasteries and their lands as the property of their families or clans. In matters of morals the church did not often intervene; marriage, for example, was a secular issue. Parishes and parish structures did not exist—and besides, the married clergy were

Above *An early Irish grave slab from Clonmacnoise. In 1552 the English garrison at Athlone looted the monastery, leaving it beyond repair.*

far too busy with their farms and families to serve them.

This cosy compromise existed from the eighth century onwards. Although not fanatically celibate, the monks were not immoral. Nor did they lack learning; in fact, they largely took over the role of the *fili*, preserving saga tales and genealogies, recording them for the first time. They also produced a large body of biblical commentary and religious verse as well as some delightful nature lyrics. The short-story writer Frank O'Connor had a soft spot for the civilization of this period, which he aptly describes as that of the "little monasteries." "The rulers of the monasteries," he writes, "having disposed of the Romantist prigs, are no longer the harsh unworldly men we meet in the pages of Bede, who read nothing but their gospels and Psalm books. They are far more like the parsons of Peacock and Meredith—wealthy, worldly, scholarly men who live in the little oases of civilization among the bogs and the woods, in comfortable wooden houses with wine cellars and libraries, with clever sons who will become in their turn abbots or professors of scripture, and clever daughters who will manage big convents or marry among the ruling classes. They are custodians of relics and treasures worth the ransom of a great many kings."

Above *A 'carpet' page from the richly decorated Book of Kells made by monks in the scriptorium of the monastery at Kells, County Meath, in the seventh century. When Queen Victoria saw the book, during a visit to Ireland, she asked for a pen, under the impression that she was expected to sign it! The book can be seen in Trinity College Library, Dublin.*

Though one can cast some doubt on the monastic wine cellars mentioned by O'Connor, there is no doubt about the treasures. These very treasures lured the Vikings to turn the Arcadian dream of Irish history into a nightmare.

The Norse raiders struck suddenly from the sea in their light, swift boats equipped with that new invention, the keel. In AD 795 they burned the church of Lambay Island off Dublin and attacked two island monasteries, Inishmurray and Inishboffin off the west coast. Why monasteries? Well, there were no towns or centers of population and the monasteries contained portable wealth in the form of relics in shrines of precious metal, decorated book shrines, and altar vessels of gold and silver.

Viking raids on island and coastal monasteries continued for about 40 years. Then the raiders began to strike more boldly inland, deep into the heart of the country, sending fleets up the Boyne, the Liffey and, above all, the Shannon. From these raids they could reach the rich monasteries of Clonmacnoise, Birr and Seir. In 840 the Vikings started to build ship shelters along the coast, and by 841 wintered for the first time in Dublin. Gradually, over two centuries, these Viking forts became the first Irish towns. The Viking towns of Stangford, Dublin, Wicklow, Wexford, Waterford, Cork and Limerick mushroomed along the east and south coasts.

Unlike their Danish brothers in England or France, where they became the civic-minded Normans, the Irish Vikings did not seek land. Instead, piracy gave way to trade and industry. Newly excavated Viking Dublin reveals industrial zones of shoemakers, combmakers, metal workers and potters. Towns and their hinterlands were the Viking sphere of influence; the largest territory they held was the coastal plain from north Dublin to Wicklow. They intermarried with Irish families, joined them in internecine warfare and, under the more harmless name of Ostmen, formed a small but important component of Irish society.

The Norse raiders gave the Irish civilization in the form of towns, coinage, and the arts of fishing and shipping. On the negative side, their violence and destruction broke up the cozy framework of Irish society. Violence replaced the restraints of society and customary law. The overlordships that developed in response to Viking attacks added a new

Above *Archeologists painstakingly uncover the remains of the tenth-century Viking settlement at Wood Quay, Dublin. The Vikings adopted the Irish name Dubh Linn (Dark Pool) for their settlement, which soon amalgamated with another Celtic settlement, Baile Atha Cliath (Town of the Hurdles), on the north bank of the Liffey.*

Above *Round towers such as this one at Ardmore in County Waterford mark many monastic sites in Ireland and probably served as bell towers. Monastic life at Ardmore began with St. Declan, whose activities predated those of St. Patrick by about 30 years.*

element of violent competitiveness to Irish society. This, in turn, never allowed any overlord to become so strong that a countrywide power could be established to resist the next challenge—that of the Normans.

During their Irish sojourn, the Ostmen of the Irish towns became Christian. When bishops were appointed, English-trained monks who owed allegiance to Canterbury were chosen rather than Irish priests. These, with a few reforming Irish bishops based in Munster, established contact with the reformist Continental church of Gregory the Great. This began a series of reforming synods in the first half of the twelfth century which took on the ambitious task of internal reform of the Irish Church. They set up a system of territorial dioceses presided over by bishops. Four metropolitan archbishoprics were created—Armagh the primacy, Dublin, Cashel and Tuam, with a series of suffragan sees under them. On paper, at least, the Irish Church assumed the form it still maintains today.

The work of reform was much helped by the introduction of the Continental orders of monks. The Cistercians were introduced into Ireland by Malachy, the saintly and reforming Bishop of Armagh, mostly through his friendship with their founder, Bernard of Clairvaux. The first foundation at Mellifont commenced in 1142 and within 50 years it had spun off 20 communities. The canons regular of St. Augustine also introduced by Malachy were even more prolific and before the end of the century the two orders between them had superseded the older Celtic monasteries.

In spite of these reforms, Rome was dissatisfied with the self-healing progress of the Irish Church. This is the only way one can interpret the action of Pope Adrian IV (the one

Above *The Cross of Muiredach at Monasterboice, County Louth, is carved with biblical scenes. Erected in the tenth century, it is considered to be one of the finest high crosses in existence.*

Left *Glendalough (Glen of Two Lakes) is a much-visited beauty spot in the Wicklow Mountains. St. Kevin's Church is named after the seventh-century hermit who founded the monastery there.*

and only English pope, as the Irish are quick to point out), who in 1155 "granted and donated Ireland" to the English King Henry II. The Pope's motives were spelled out by his intimate friend and fellow countryman John of Salisbury: "In response to my petition the Pope granted and donated Ireland to the illustrious English King, Henry II, to be held by him and his successors as his letters still testify. He did this by that right of longstanding from the Donation of Constantine whereby all islands are said to belong to the Roman Church. Through me the Pope sent a gold ring set with a magnificent emerald as a sign that he had invested the King with the right to rule Ireland; it was later ordered that this ring be kept in the public treasury."

Irish historians have frequently thrown doubt on the very existence, not to say validity, of the papal bull *Laudabiliter*, which was reputed to give formal expression to this arbitrary gift to an English king by an English pope. Whatever the legal facts, certainly this feeling of the necessity of reforming the Irish was held not only in England but in Rome. Even a favorable witness like Bernard of Clairvaux felt that something must be done about Ireland. Writing about Malachy's task in Ireland, Bernard says: "Never had he found men so shameless in their morals, so wild in their rites, so impious in their faith, so barbarous in their laws, so stubborn in discipline, so unclean in their life. They were Christians in name; in fact they were pagans. They did not give first fruits or tithes; they did not enter on lawful marriage; they made no confessions; nowhere was there to be found any who might either seek or impose penance. Ministers of the altar were few indeed. But what need was there of more when even the few lived idle lives among the laity."

That Bernard was overstating his case we can gather from the contrast he describes when Malachy set fruitfully to work: "Churches were rebuilt and a clergy appointed to them: the sacraments were duly solemnized and confessions were made: the people came to church, and those who were living in concubinage were united in lawful wedlock." That was the intention, but the record shows that a long time was to pass before such an orderly

Far left *The first Cistercian monastery in Ireland was founded by St. Malachy at Mellifont, County Louth, in 1142. This is the octagonal lavabo where the monks washed.*

Left *St. Brendan founded a monastery at Clonfert, County Galway, in the sixth century, but the present cathedral dates from the twelfth. The west doorway is decorated with carvings of human heads and marigolds.*

Above *Cormac's Chapel, built in the twelfth century, is the oldest surviving building on the Rock of Cashel, County Tipperary. The Rock, a limestone outcrop, rears up from the surrounding plainland. Legend has it that the Devil, flying overhead with a stone in his mouth, dropped it when he saw St. Patrick below him.*

Right *Brian Boru was crowned in 977 at 'Royal and Saintly Cashel,' stronghold of the kings of Munster. Tradition has it that St. Patrick stopped here to baptize a Munster king, and also that he plucked a shamrock leaf from the hillside to illustrate the doctrine of the Holy Trinity.*

Below The Marriage of Strongbow and Aoife *by the Victorian painter Daniel Maclise shows the King of Leinster marrying his daughter to the Earl of Pembroke in order to secure the military assistance of the Normans. (National Gallery of Ireland)*

Above *Gerald of Wales (Giraldus Cambrensis), who visited Ireland shortly after the Norman invasion, thought the Irish a barbaric people. This illustration from his manuscript* The History and Topography of Ireland *shows the making of a book at Kildare. (British Library)*

state was achieved.

In fact the Norman arrival in Ireland had little to do with church reform. The Normans simply took sides for mercenary motives in an Irish domestic quarrel.

Dermot MacMurrough, the King of Leinster, found himself on the losing side in an Irish tribal fight with the O'Connor overlords of Connaught and particularly with one of O'Connor's henchmen, Tighernan O'Rourke, whose wife MacMurrough had kidnapped in a previous campaign. He fled abroad and sought help from Henry II of England. In spite of his grants and bulls from the Pope, Henry showed little interest. Instead he referred Dermot to some of his underemployed Welsh knights, in particular Richard de Clare, Earl of Pembroke (known to Irish history as Strongbow), and to a wild Norman-Welsh clan, "the sons of Nesta," who became the Geraldines of Irish history. Strongbow was bribed by Dermot MacMurrough with the offer of his daughter's hand in marriage and succession to the rich kingdom of Leinster.

Small forces of Norman knights, Welsh archers and Flemish mercenaries trickled quietly into Ireland. Strongbow himself arrived with the main force in August 1170 and soon retook Leinster for Dermot and captured the Ostmen's capital of Dublin. With Dermot's death in 1171 he was able to claim his inheritance as King of Leinster.

Henry II at last began to show interest in Ireland when he realized that Strongbow and his companions might set up an independent kingdom there. In 1171 he arrived in person to claim the allegiance of his knights and of any of the Irish kings who felt inclined to submit to him, which many did. Churchmen also tendered their loyalty and were rewarded with his encouragement in reforming synods. The Norman invasion of Ireland was now official. This was not, however, a Norman Conquest. Because of the peculiar decentralized nature of Irish administration there was no single overall authority to conquer.

For the next two centuries Norman power fluctuated in Ireland. At its strongest, two-thirds of the country came, directly or indirectly, under Norman sway. But even then that power was exercised only in the Ostman ports, in new towns like New Ross and Kilkenny which had been set up in the river

Right *William Marshall founded Tintern Abbey in County Wexford in 1200 in thanks for a safe crossing from England. The first monks were Welsh Cistercians from the parent abbey in Monmouthshire. After the dissolution of the monasteries in the sixteenth century, part of the abbey was converted into a three-storey house which was inhabited until 1963.*

Above *The magnificent medieval Great Hall at Desmond Castle, Newcastle West, County Limerick, once the home of the Desmond Geraldines.*

Above *The ruins of another Cistercian monastery at Jerpoint, County Kilkenny. The twelfth-century abbey nave and the later tower are seen here from the fifteenth-century cloisters.*

Right *Within a few years of arriving in Ireland, the Normans began to build massive stone fortresses. This is Trim Castle on the banks of the River Boyne in County Meath, started by Hugh de Lacy in 1180.*

valleys, and in the advanced castles and garrisons in the west, like Galway and Athenry. Ireland was divided into two societies: the castle and town society of the Normans with its Norman-French language and English law, and a traditional rural society with the Irish language and brehon law.

Intermarriage and contact with the Irish led many Normans to adopt Irish clothes, speech and customs. A parliament held at Kilkenny in 1366 set out to correct these abuses, bewailing the fact that "now many English of the said land, forsaking the English language, fashion, manner of riding, laws and usages, live and govern themselves by the manners, fashions and language of the Irish enemy, and have made divers marriages and alliances between themselves and the Irish enemies by which the said land and its liege people, the English language and the allegiance due to our lord the King and the English laws are put in subjection and decayed..."

In spite of such laws, which were many times repeated, commerce between the two nations continued but they never became one. In spite of the oft-repeated phrase about becoming "more Irish than the Irish themselves," the Normans did not become Irish, nor did they succeed in conquering the Irish. Ireland was now two nations and so in many ways it has continued.

The effects of the Norman invasion are visible even today on the Irish landscape. The Normans were not casual raiders or founders of trading posts as their Viking predecessors were; their objective was land and stability. They held the land they captured by building castles. At first these castles were temporary affairs, high mounds of earth topped by wooden forts, the motte and bailey of the Bayeux tapestry. Soon, though, they were of stone. In the heart of Dublin, on the sea coast in Carrickfergus, on a rock overlooking Limerick harbor and above all in the river valleys of Leinster, walled enclosures with drum towers at the corners and often a high circular or square keep in

Above *New Ross on the River Barrow was one of several towns founded by the Normans in the river valleys of southeast Ireland.*

the middle were raised in the green and flat Irish landscape. They dominated whole plains, as the great castle of Trim does in County Meath. They stood at river crossings, as at Bunratty in County Clare.

Under the shelter of these castles, Norman towns grew up with mills and markets. Great churches of the new Continental orders were built in the towns. The abbeys of Duiske and Tintern in the Leinster river valleys were as English in their style as the monks that came from the English mother houses. Indeed the very stone for their vaults and window dressings was imported from Dundry, near Bristol, and floated on flat boats up the Irish rivers.

Even where they could not possess the land, the Normans claimed it, fiefed it under their feudal system to their supporters—or even to the Irish who actually possessed it—for knights' fee, service and rent. If they could collect, well and good; if not, they at least had their claim on paper. The Irish, with their own laws decreeing that lands should be held in common by the family or tribe rather than claimed by individuals, understood little and cared even less for the legal tangle in which they became enmeshed.

In the fourteenth century there was an Irish resurgence. The Irish, with the help of mercenaries from Scotland with their long axes, were learning to fight back. The area of Ireland actually controlled by the English government contracted to the Pale, an area of a few counties in Leinster around Dublin.

In the rest of the country the Irish chieftains were building themselves castles, of the tall, rectangular type with bristling battlements that had come into fashion. Like the Normans, they too were endowing abbeys. Increasingly, the new religious foundations were friaries of the mendicant orders—Franciscans, Dominicans and Augustinians—which had begun to replace the old monastic orders in influence. The slim friary bell-towers, with their characteristic Irish inward slope or "batter," and the empty triangle of their roof gables rose in the western sky far away from any town or village.

From 1400 on, the Norman settlement in Ireland went into decline. English kings were too involved in Europe to spare money for an

Below *The three-tiered nave of the Anglo-Norman St. Patrick's Cathedral in Dublin.*

Right *The two-storey round keep at Dundrum Castle, County Down, was probably built late in the twelfth century.*

Far left *Donsoghly Castle in north County Dublin is owned by the Office of Public Works.*

Left *The O'Brien castle of Leamaneh, County Clare, consists of fifteenth-century tower with a four-storey mansion built on two centuries later.*

Below *The ruins of Quin Abbey, County Clare, founded by Franciscan monks in 1433.*

Irish colony and the Wars of the Roses finally withdrew attention from Ireland.

As so often before, it was one of the great Norman families that filled the power vacuum. Early in the century, James Butler, the fourth Earl of Ormonde, held sway. He ruled the rich lands of Tipperary and Kilkenny and, like all Butlers, was prominent in diplomacy and negotiation rather than battle. He was definitely a king's man. When he died in 1452, his son and heir married an English noblewoman and identified his interests with England, and so the Butlers disappeared from Irish history for a long time. The next family that came to power were the Geraldines of Desmond, the southern branch of the legendary "family of Nesta." They ruled all Munster like a Gaelic kingdom, having not only feudal loyalty from Norman families such as the Barrys and the Roches and from junior Geraldines like the knights of Glin

Right *The three Lakes of Killarney became a tourist attraction in the mid-eighteenth century. The local landowner, Lord Kenmare, quick to spot the opportunities offered by travellers in search of romantic scenery, granted many new leases for houses and inns in the area.*

and Kerry, but also recognition from such great Gaelic families as the MacCarthys and O'Sullivans. Thomas, the seventh Earl of Desmond, was more a Gaelic chief than a Norman lord. He held sway from 1461 to 1467, when he was arrested, detained and beheaded. This act drove the Desmond family into rebellion against the crown which continued for the best part of a century. The rebellion was finally defeated under Elizabeth I.

It was now the turn of the Fitzgeralds of Kildare. Garret Mor, the great Earl of Kildare, came to power in 1477 and, through favor and disfavor, continued in power until the eve of the Tudor reconquest of Ireland in 1513.

The Norman settlers had fixed their towns and castles in the plains, along the sea coasts and in the rich accessible river valleys; the highlands, the bogs, the forests and the rich pastures beyond the forests were still Gaelic country offering no loyalty to the English crown. It was these disloyal lands that the Tudor monarchs set out to conquer. They used new methods: surveyors and maps, and transplantation instead of feudal grants. They were motivated by religion, by the English Reformation in Ireland, as well as by Tudor colonial expansionism.

Above *This woodcut by John Derricke, from his* Image of Irelande *(1581), shows Sir Henry Sidney, one of Elizabeth I's deputies in Ireland, leaving Dublin Castle for a tour of the country. The heads displayed above the gate are a warning to would-be rebels.*

The two Irish nations—the Norman settlers and the Gaelic clans—now had common cause in a besieged religion. The last parliament in Kilkenny, the Confederation of Kilkenny of 1642, tried to unite against the Puritan parliament. The Duke of Ormonde was, as always, keeping a watchful eye on proceedings, but Oliver Cromwell brought them to a murderous close. The Duke of Ormonde surfaced again as Viceroy after the Restoration, but the Gaelic part of Ireland, landless and proscribed by ruthless penal laws, entered the long dark of the hidden Ireland.

Right *The River Foyle at Derry looks peaceful enough in the light of evening. But during the three-month siege of Derry in 1689 the city's 30,000 inhabitants were reduced to eating dogs, cats, mice, candles and leather.*

From Cromwell to Parnell 3

Liam de Paor

Cromwell's soldiers conquered a country that was already devastated by war, famine and plague. His civil administrators followed through with a religious policy that was directed in part against the Anglican prelacy, but much more fiercely against the Roman Catholic clergy, who were hunted down. Many were killed.

This period of government under the Protectorate left memories which endured among the ordinary people for many generations. They had to practice their religion in many places by stealth, gathering at "mass rocks" in out of the way places, protected by lookouts. In the popular memory, the days of Cromwellian persecution were ultimately transferred to a later period, so that the whole episode came to be associated with the penal laws against Catholicism enacted during the eighteenth century. The name of Cromwell passed into folklore as a great bogey.

The Protectorate carried out very extensive confiscations of land—the war had been financed by promising confiscated land to those who took part in it. Large numbers of "delinquent" proprietors were moved across the Shannon to Connacht and Clare, there receiving estates equivalent to a proportion of the lands they had to leave in the east.

This plantation scheme, under the Act of Settlement, was only partly successful. Its administrators had so much trouble trying to find out who owned what land where (so that they could redistribute it) that they were forced to attempt an accurate survey. The result was the "Down Survey," the first detailed mapping of Ireland.

One of the destabilizing features of Irish politics throughout the seventeenth century was the great uneasiness of almost all landlords about the security of their tenure. At a time when common people had little say, if any, in politics, and when the conduct of government and the formulation of policy was in the hands of the landed gentry and aristocracy, the widespread uncertainty created by repeated confiscations was probably the largest single influence on the political decisions made by the landlords.

After the death of Cromwell in 1658, politicians in England decided to bring back the king, Charles II, son of the king whom Cromwell had fought and put to death. This immediately raised crucial questions about land ownership. Were the dispossessed and often exiled lords who had been faithful to the crown to get their lands back? Were the Cromwellians who had been given land under the plantation to lose it again? The Restoration of 1660 was based on an attempt at a compromise between

Above *In the latter part of the seventeenth century French Huguenot craftsmen settled in Dublin, followed by the Dutch and Flemish, who introduced buildings of brick. This Huguenot cemetery is in Merrion Row, Dublin.*

Above *Cromwell crossed to Ireland in 1649 to subdue the last remaining supporters of Charles I and the Royalist cause. During his attack on Catholic Drogheda, the garrison, the clergy and many townspeople were massacred. This eighteenth-century engraving by Barlow shows Cromwell directing the attack.*

the two.

This was more difficult in Ireland than in England. Almost every landlord was left with one kind of grievance or another. In the immediate post-Cromwellian period the old Gaelic order that had survived for a thousand years finally disintegrated. Contemporary Irish writing is full of anger and lament for the passing of the old order. Only a few of the ancient great families—those that had become Protestant—remained in possession of extensive estates, although some of the lesser old Catholic landlords still hung on here and there (the O'Connells, in Kerry, being a good example).

When Charles II died and was succeeded by his brother, James II, in 1685, the effect on Ireland was immediate and disturbing. James was a Roman Catholic and his accession to the throne raised Catholic hopes for a restoration of confiscated lands and estates, and correspondingly gave rise to Protestant fears of losing the same lands. In 1687 James appointed a Catholic, Richard Talbot, Duke of Tyrconnell, as his Lord Lieutenant to govern Ireland. Tyrconnell was a known opponent of the compromise settlement which left the Protestant planters in possession of the lands and began replacing Protestants with Catholics in the public service and recruiting Catholics in large numbers into the army. He made it clear that he proposed to undo the settlement. However in the "Glorious Revolution" of 1688 another English rebellion, this time bloodless, overthrew the king, who fled to France, and brought in his place his daughter Mary (a Protestant) and her husband William of Orange. This was stimulated by the birth of a male heir to the throne, opening the way to a Catholic dynasty. Tyrconnell, however, held Ireland for James.

But not quite all of it. Here and there Protes-

Below *A floodlit Treaty Stone beside the River Shannon at Limerick commemorates the Treaty of Limerick in 1691, which put an end to hostilities, though not to resentments, between Williamites and Jacobites.*

Left *The streets of the county town of Wexford are peaceful today, but once they ran with blood. Cromwell's troops slaughtered at least 2000 inhabitants.*

tant landowners and settlers acted against him, especially in Ulster. Derry and Enniskillen closed their gates against him.

Ireland now became a battlefield in a European war, for the king of France decided to give military support to James II against William III. James landed in the south of Ireland in March 1689 and marched north to Derry, whose governor, Robert Lundy, was just about to open the gates to him when he was overthrown from within the city. The siege of Derry lasted for three months and was finally lifted when relief ships got through to the starving population and garrison. It has become one of the great legends of Ulster loyalism.

Soon after the raising of the siege, Marshal Schomberg, King William's commander, landed at Belfast Lough and made a base for the winter at Carrickfergus. In the spring of 1690, 7000 French troops landed in the south to aid King James. In June, King William landed at Carrickfergus and joined Schomberg. They marched south and were met by King James and his forces at the River Boyne, 30

Below *Jan Wyck's* Battle of the Boyne, *painted in 1693, now hangs in the National Gallery of Ireland.*

miles north of Dublin, on July 1 (July 12 in our present calendar). Schomberg was killed as he crossed the river, but James, defeated, fled to Dublin, which he soon had to abandon. The war went on for a year, with the Jacobites holding and defending the south and west. After their defeat in the critical battle of Aughrim (County Galway) in 1691, they were besieged in Limerick and finally surrendered, on terms, in October. The military terms of the treaty of Limerick were implemented, but the Protestant parliament which met in Dublin refused to ratify the civil terms.

Instead they proceeded to build a system designed to exclude Roman Catholics from property, power and influence, and also to put pressure on them to accept and conform to the Protestant faith. Further confiscations of land continued until the opening years of the eighteenth century. By then, more than 80 percent of Irish land had changed hands within about a hundred years, and in the process a whole new class of proprietors gained control of the property and power of the country, without roots in the past. This was what became known as the "Protestant Ascendancy."

Above *The lush Boyne Valley in County Meath was the site of James II's defeat by William of Orange in 1690.*

The parliament passed a series of laws, known as the "Popery laws" or "penal laws," to restrict to Anglican Protestants the power, property and privilege of the country. Test oaths excluded Catholics and Presbyterians from most public offices. The Roman Catholic Church received no recognition of any kind—it became, as it were, invisible to the constitution—but various prohibitions and tests were directed at those who confessed its faith. Inheritable property was restricted to Protestants. Catholics could own property but were obliged to subdivide it among their children on death. Many Catholic landowning families converted to Protestantism to save their estates intact; many others sank in the world as sub-

Right *The rigorous formality of a state ball at Dublin Castle depicted by an anonymous eighteenth-century artist. By the end of the seventeenth century the majority of Irish land was in the hands of the Protestant Ascendancy.*

division broke up their estates. There were numerous irritating or humiliating rules; a Catholic, for example, could not own a horse worth more than £5.

In spite of prolonged warfare, the Irish population had been increasing in the later seventeenth century, and by 1700 amounted probably to about 2 million people. Three-quarters or more of these were Roman Catholics, but after Limerick there was no way that the old Catholic ruling class—including both the ancient Gaelic families and families descended from medieval Norman or English settlers—could command power in the land.

In Ulster there was a considerable Protestant population, apart from the "Ascendancy." This derived partly from the Plantation of nearly a century earlier, partly from the dense early seventeenth-century settlement of parts of Antrim and Down by Scottish Presbyterians, and partly from an equally important migration late in the seventeenth century.

New Protestant towns had been established in connection with the Plantation. Most of these soon numbered Catholics as well as Protestants in their population. It is common to find, in surveys of the time, "Scotch," "English" and "Irish" quarters or streets in the towns. The countryside was similarly mixed. But Ulster had acquired a character markedly different from that of the rest of the country. By the early eighteenth century observers (including Jonathan Swift, dean of St. Patrick's Cathedral in Dublin) were remarking that Ulster was the only part of Ireland that didn't look miserable and backward.

Parts of the country, mainly in the east and in the old colonial towns, had been English-speaking for centuries. English was now the language of law, government, trade and all kinds of public discourse throughout Ireland. It was the language of the new Ascendancy. It was also, although sometimes in dialect forms (including Scottish), the language of the Ulster Protestant settlement. But a large part of the Catholic population in parts of the east as well as most of the west was still Irish-speaking.

In spite of the breakdown of their old social order, there flourished in the Irish-speaking areas of the eighteenth century a lively

Above The 2nd Lord Aldburgh reviewing the Volunteers in Belan Park, *painted by Francis Wheatley in 1781, is one of a series of large works commemorating the activities of the Volunteers. The Volunteers were formed to defend Ireland while the British were away fighting in America.*

Left *Jonathan Swift (1667-1745) was the Anglican dean of St. Patrick's Cathedral in Dublin and the author of* Gulliver's Travels. *He wrote various pamphlets and the famous satire* A Modest Proposal, *in which he drew attention to the appalling conditions of the poor in Ireland. (National Portrait Gallery, London)*

literature, produced by poets who no longer had the elaborate formal training of their medieval predecessors, but who composed poems in more popular forms. As the century wore on, many of these turned to schoolteaching, providing instruction in reading, writing (in English) and arithmetic—and often much more—for the children of Catholic tenant farmers and the like. Some of these schools were in makeshift shelters, and the whole system came to be known as "hedge-schools." When all the publicly recognized schools, whether in receipt of public or of private grants, were purveyors of Protestantism as well as literacy, the hedge-schools, however makeshift, were clung to by the Catholic population as a means of acquiring education without compromising their beliefs. Some of them taught a radical dissent from both the political and the religious principles of the State, and the country schoolmaster was gradually, through changing systems and changing times, to become one of the most important transmitters of nationalist sentiments.

The Ascendancy functioned politically through its parliament in Dublin, which met more regularly in the eighteenth century than in the seventeenth. There was an implicit bargain that the Ascendancy would maintain the English interest in Ireland, while in return the British government would secure the Ascendancy's privilege. Within the scope of this broad understanding there was room for much difference of view. Attempts by the Dublin parliament to argue for its rights as the parliament of a distinct kingdom under the same crown as England were met by a Declaratory Act which asserted the subordination of the Irish parliament to Westminster. There was much friction in economic matters, mainly because of British restrictions on Irish trade. In a particularly heated dispute over a British grant of authority to a Birmingham coiner to strike coins for Ireland—which were objected to for their quality and quantity—Swift published some rousing pamphlets objecting to the British government's view of its relationship with Ireland.

After the middle of the century the Irish colony began to show increasing signs of strain.

Left *In December 1796 a fleet of 35 French ships full of troops anchored in Bantry Bay off the southwest coast of Ireland. With their assistance the United Irishmen hoped to stage a revolution that would unite Catholics and Protestants and lead to the formation of an Irish republic.*

Above *James Gandon's elegant Custom House stands on Custom House Quay on the north bank of the River Liffey in Dublin. Built in 1781, the building was badly damaged by fire in 1921 during the Civil War.*

There had been a very severe famine in the 1740s, causing much death and suffering in the west, but the population, though checked briefly by this, was growing. The landlords' "improvements," through enclosures, road-building and, in some cases, the introduction of new agricultural methods, contributed to social unrest—what suited the landlords frequently disturbed their tenants. Rural secret societies began to be active, initially among Protestant tenants in the north, but soon in other parts of the country as well. The situation was eased somewhat for a while by emigration on a considerable scale. Much of this was from Ulster or the more prosperous parts of the other provinces, and it played an important part in

Above *Florence Court in County Fermanagh, one of the most beautiful houses in Ulster, was built by Lord Mount Florence in 1764. Badly damaged by fire in 1955, it has since been restored by the National Trust.*

Left *James Gandon was also the architect of the Four Courts, another of Dublin's great Georgian public buildings. Begun in 1786, it was completed in 1802. This view is from the Merchant's Quay, on the south bank of the river.*

the settlement of North America.

When the American colonies revolted, the Irish Ascendancy had very mixed feelings. It was committed to the defense of Ireland against Britain's enemies, notably France, but it had much sympathy for the insurgent Americans, colonists whose problems and grievances in many ways resembled their own. They formed a Volunteer force to help defend Irish shores, since the British needed so many soldiers for the American war, but they soon began to use the Volunteers for other purposes, including a challenge to the British government on the issue of the relationship between the two parliaments. The British, in difficulties, repealed the acts which gave offence, and the Irish legislature became independent in 1782. Although the British retained executive powers and continued as before to "manage" as best they could the Dublin parliament—persuading it to vote for most of the measures they required—the independent Irish parliament became known as "Grattan's parliament," from Henry Grattan, the chief spokesman of the "patriots," or Irish, as distinct from the British.

The arrangement soon became, from the British point of view, dangerously unworkable. There were new problems caused by the French Revolution and a new kind of war with France—an ideological war. Many people in the British Isles had sympathy, initially at least, with the revolution and its objectives, and much political excitement was generated. Political societies of radical democratic views

Right *This is the elegant facade of the Bank of Ireland, once Parliament House, the meeting place of the Irish parliament. Begun in 1728, it was the first edifice in the world purpose-built as a parliament. It was sold to the Bank of Ireland after the Act of Union in 1800. The present Irish parliament sits in the Dáil, Leinster House.*

Far right *Dunboy Castle, near Castletownberehaven in County Cork, was originally a fifteenth-century building erected on the site of an even earlier position of defense.*

were formed and became an object of concern to the government. In Ireland an organization was formed shortly after the outbreak of the French Revolution, the United Irishmen. One of its most active founder-members was Theobald Wolfe Tone, a young man of adventurous character who had developed radical and revolutionary ideas.

Such societies were formed elsewhere too, but in Ireland they soon impinged on the activities and membership of the agrarian secret societies which had been active, on and off, since soon after the middle of the century. The activities of the "Whiteboys," in Tipperary and neighboring counties, in about 1760 had amounted to a virtual rebellion. In south Ulster conflict had developed between rival Catholic and Protestant secret societies. The Catholics had a widespread organization known as the "Defenders." The Protestants, in 1795, formed the Orange Order after a bloody affray with the Defenders. The United Irishmen, forced underground as they became more radical in their ideas, committed to a republic, drew upon the Defenders' organization to broaden their movement.

The government, through its numerous spies and informers, was well informed about these developments, and in 1797 and 1798 moved against the conspirators who planned a French Revolution in Ireland. Soldiers moved into the most dangerously disaffected areas (mostly in Ulster), searching houses, flogging and inflicting other punishments, often to the death, and generally intimidating all who might have felt inclined to show sympathy, actively or passively, to rebellion. Government agents also arrested many of the planners and organizers of insurrection. In spite of this, or because these measures goaded some people into rash action, there were scattered and uncoordinated, but formidable, uprisings in many parts of Ireland in the summer of 1798. Fighting was bloody—perhaps as many as 50,000 people died in it. But the rebellions were crushed and terrible reprisals followed.

The British government, headed by William Pitt, now decided to put into operation a system that it had already decided was the only way to cope with the Irish problem. Expending a

Right *A typical Georgian street in Dublin. Georgian Dublin, centered on Merrion Square and Fitzwilliam Square, is a pattern of squares and linking terraces, with many intriguing variations in the design of windows, doors, fanlights and railings.*

Left *The rising led by Robert Emmet in 1803 was more of a street riot than a rebellion. This engraving by George Cruikshank depicts the murder of Lord Kilwarden in Dublin.*

Below *The Brazen Head, Bridge Street, near the River Liffey, is one of Dublin's oldest pubs. Robert Emmet hid here for several weeks before he was caught and executed.*

remarkable amount of money and patronage, even by eighteenth-century standards, they persuaded the Dublin parliament to vote for its own extinction and pushed through the British parliament an Act of Union, which came into operation on the first day of the new century, January 1, 1801. On that day the United Kingdom of Great Britain and Ireland came into existence. Ireland ceased to have a parliament, but was to elect 100 Members of Parliament to the House of Commons in Westminster and contribute a number of peers and bishops to the House of Lords too.

Many members of the Protestant Ascendancy were dismayed at the loss of their colonial parliament through which, to some extent, they had been able to manage their own affairs. Members of the parliament, who shared this dismay but had been persuaded to overcome their feelings, were handsomely compensated. Many of the leaders of Catholic opinion, such as they were, were tepidly pleased with the Union, since they had been given to understand that the remaining restrictions on Catholic participation in political life would be removed after the Union. But opposition to this in Britain was too strong and the restrictions remained.

Further, the Union, in the course of a generation or two, began to appear to Protestants as the surest guarantee of their position, while Catholics had a growing sense of grievance. The pressure for parliamentary reform was changing, or threatening to change, the political balance. Numbers, majorities, counted much more than in the past. And in Ireland the already overwhelming Catholic majority appeared to be increasing, while in the United Kingdom as a whole Catholics were in a minority. The agitation for Catholic emancipation that began soon after the Union was passed was conducted initially by lobbying, which was unsuccessful. Then Daniel O'Connell, a young Catholic lawyer from a family of Kerry landowners, organized a very different kind of agitation.

He led a nationwide "Catholic Association," with two tiers of membership, to which people all over the country contributed a regular subscription in guineas or pennies. The Catholic clergy were *ex officio* members and looked after the organization at parish level. Within a few years O'Connell presided over something uniquely new in politics, a non-violent political

machine based on the mobilization of a mass democratic movement. In 1829, through the weight of its numbers, it eventually effected the introduction of a bill allowing Catholics to enter parliament at Westminster.

In due course O'Connell began another agitation, in some ways more impressive than the first, for repeal of the Act of Union. Under the Union, northeastern Ireland had developed economically and rapidly. A textile industry, based on the old linen industry but soon encompassing the manufacture of cotton cloth, had grown up in the area around Lisburn and Belfast. Moving from home to mill production and machine manufacture, this part of Ireland became involved in the social and economic changes occurring in England's northeast and Midlands, in the "Industrial Revolution." The rest of Ireland failed to flourish in this way. The country was nearly ungovernable, largely because of deficiencies in the landholding system itself and in the social structures it supported.

The landlords remained, for the most part, in the view of their tenants, alien imposters. The social cement that should have held the gentry and the rest of the rural population together with some sense of mutual obligation was very thin indeed. Absenteeism was common; subdivision of holdings and other practices made estate management very difficult; and the evil of "rack-renting," which included penalizing the tenant for improvements, was widespread. Violence was endemic, most of it localized and concerned with matters such as rents, the bitterly resented tithe (a tax for the maintenance of ministers of the established church) and the fees exacted from the people for the support of their own priests. These smoldering grievances were from time to time

Far left *Thatched cottages are as common as sheep in the fields of Ireland. This one nestles by the sea near Derrybeg, County Donegal.*

Left *Mount Stewart House, County Down, was built in the eighteenth century. The gardens occupy 80 acres and contain many rare plants, shrubs and trees.*

Below A View of Sackville Street *(now O'Connell Street), Dublin, by Michael Angelo Hayes. Nelson Pillar dominates the scene, with the colonnades of the General Post Office on the left. (National Gallery of Ireland)*

given a wider political meaning and also added weight by the rapid increase in the size of the population, which rose from about 5 million in 1800 to considerably more than 8 million in 1841 (in spite of considerable emigration to Britain and North America).

To repeal the Union in such circumstances would—so it seemed to most Protestants in particular—have led to disaster. There was very little support for the proposal in the British parliament and an articulate opposition to it developed in Ulster. O'Connell himself appeared to use the repeal agitation partly as a means of putting pressure on the government to yield more reforms in Ireland. For a short time it seemed that this tactic might succeed: the

agitation was muted, the government made some small attempts to meet Irish grievances and the level of violence dropped sharply. Then, with a change of administration, this process ended, and in the early 1840s O'Connell organized and led his vast army of beggars in an extraordinary political campaign. He summoned and addressed enormous mass meetings, some of them held at places of great romantic and historic interest (such as Tara). When he announced a meeting for Clontarf, on the outskirts of Dublin, however, the government banned it and O'Connell called it off. It was difficult, without any body of support in parliament, to see where he could go from there. He himself was growing old and increas-

Left *Charles Stewart Parnell (1846-1891) dominated British parliamentary life in the 1880s, putting Irish Home Rule firmly on the Irish and British political agenda. A divorce scandal brought his career to an untimely end. This statue stands at the top of O'Connell Street, pointing toward the Rotunda, in 1752 the first purpose-built maternity hospital in Europe.*

Below *A potato field in the west of Ireland. Over the centuries, hunger and poverty forced many thousands of country people to abandon such farms and take ship to America.*

Below *The prolonged famine of the 1840s caused widespread starvation and homelessness. Those who had, gave. In this engraving a girl distributes clothes to the poor from the back of a cart at Kilrush, County Clare.*

ingly in conflict with an organization of young men—known as "Young Ireland"—who were romantic nationalists. Originally his supporters, they romanticized war and violence and thought he deferred too much to Catholic, rather than secular Irish or national, interests.

These events were overtaken by the major disaster of the 1840s, remembered in Ireland, because of its scale, as "the Famine" (although there had been other famines). Blight destroyed the potato crop, the food on which more than half the population lived. It appeared widely in 1845 and everywhere in 1846. In 1847 seed potatoes were not sown. Tens of thousands of

people starved to death. The hunger was followed by epidemics of disease that claimed more hundreds of thousands of lives. Dreadful scenes were witnessed, especially in the overcrowded squatters' potato patches in the west of Ireland. After the famine there was a great tide of emigration, almost all of it to North America, and the tide continued for years. The population fell sharply and went on falling for the rest of the century.

The government was hampered in its handling of this calamity both by the inadequacy of its administrative machinery and, much more, by prevailing preconceived ideas on political

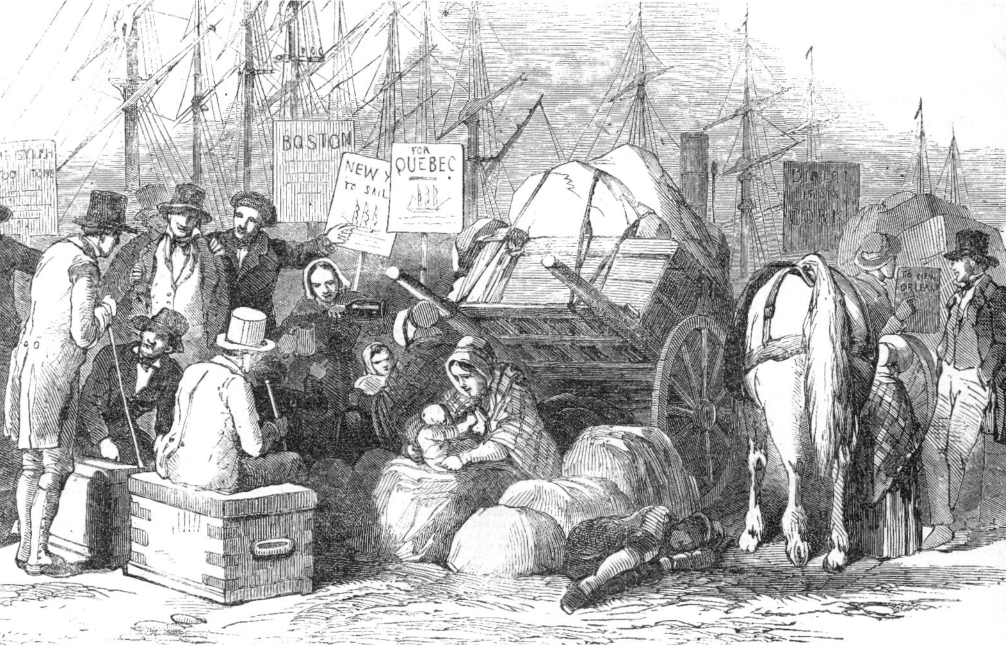

economy. A reluctance to interfere or compete with market forces resulted in no direct government intervention, except when it was too late for many of the starving people. The emigrants carried overseas with them a hatred of British rule (which they blamed) that was to persist for generations.

Above *A group of emigrants, surrounded by their belongings, wait for a boat to take them to a new life on the other side of the Atlantic.*

In the wake of the famine some of the Young Irelanders attempted to improvise an uprising. This was a total failure but it helped to commit a section of Irish political opinion, opposed to the Union, to conspiratorial organization and the use of armed force. Within another generation a more formidable organization on such lines was created—the Fenians—whose Irish Republican Brotherhood, sworn to the achievement of an independent Irish republic, was to persist into the twentieth century as a small but stubborn body, with the potential for re-establishing a large-scale organization. The Fenians also attempted an uprising, in 1867, but it came to nothing.

But a different kind of revolution began to

Right *In the late 1870s another famine threatened and once again families unable to pay the rent were evicted from their homes. This photograph was taken in County Clare in the 1880s.*

brew toward the end of the nineteenth century, the result of the conjunction of several powerful forces. One was the political organization of masses of people, of the kind pioneered by O'Connell. Agitation for "home rule"—for an assembly in Ireland with some limited powers of government in purely Irish affairs —was led by Charles Stewart Parnell, a County Wicklow landlord. He succeeded in bringing a group of Irish MPs at Westminster under tight party discipline and mounted a campaign that made full use of the Irish advantage (when they had it) of holding the balance of power between Liberals and Conservatives. These tactics were successful to the extent that two Home Rule bills were introduced, in 1886 and 1893. Although both were defeated (in different ways), Home Rule had been made a central issue in British politics and was to continue so.

Another force, partly marshalled by the same Parnell and partly by others such as Michael Davitt, was the agrarian malaise that had intermittently smoldered into violence for two centuries. Organization on a national scale, working together with political agitation and parliamentary activity, led to a series of government concessions in the form of land purchase and other land bills. By the beginning of the twentieth century a great social revolution was in progress: transfer of land from land-

Below *Michael Davitt MP, painted here by William Orpen, agitated for rent reductions and an end to evictions. Together, he and Parnell launched the Land League. (Municipal Gallery, Dublin)*

owners to tenants, under government pressure and supervision.

The third force was that of the Fenians and their successors: armed conspiracy to overthrow the British State in Ireland. This remained in the background while the revolution in land ownership was accomplished, but its presence played some part in the events of this time.

Home Rule was defeated in the nineteenth century with the aid of industrialized Protestant Ulster, which had undergone a divergent development. It was also checked by the personal tragedy of Parnell, the result of his involvement in a divorce case. Gladstone, the British Liberal Prime Minister with whom he had worked, called on the Irish party to rid itself of a leader who was morally unacceptable. Parnell refused to go, the party split, and the Catholic Church joined Parnell's opponents. Then Parnell died, leaving an atmosphere of bitterness that caused many young people to turn away from "politics."

They turned instead to cultural matters, to the revival and organization of traditional Irish games, to the study and attempted revival of the Irish language, and to the development of ideas of an "Irish Ireland." This turning aside was to prove, in the long run, to be far more potent politics than "politics."

Right *The ruins of the General Post Office in Sackville Street (now O'Connell Street), Dublin, after the Easter Rising of 1916. This photograph was taken from Nelson Pillar, which was itself blown up in 1966.*

Far right *Maud Gonne, famed beauty, talented actress and 'political agitator.'*

Twentieth-century Ireland 4

Terence Brown

In 1902 Dublin was stirred into controversy by the first performance of a play by the poet W.B. Yeats. *Cathleen Ni Houlihan* summoned Ireland's young men to the ancient cause of rebellion against the foreign usurper. In a moment of brilliant theatricality before the final curtain the little old woman who has mysteriously visited a peasant cottage to issue this summons is transformed into a beautiful young girl with "the walk of a queen." One man who saw the performance reckoned such plays should not be produced "unless one was prepared for people to go out to shoot and be shot." The actress who played the part of the little old woman was Maud Gonne, whom a contemporary newspaper described as "the well-known political agitator." A famed beauty, she was the unattainable object of Yeats' undying ardour, a fanatically committed nationalist, the daughter of a British army officer of Irish descent and an English mother. In her own person she embodied many of the contradictions and complexities of Ireland in the twentieth century. Half-English, appearing in a play by an Irish Protestant, fomenting a rebellion that would threaten her own class, she managed in a moment of magnificent gesture to catch the imagination of a nation.

It was the image of Cathleen Ni Houlihan that a decade or so later was to work on the

imagination of a generation of poets, theorists and dreamers who recklessly declared the Republic of Ireland at the Post Office in Dublin at Easter 1916. Cathleen Ni Houlihan's image—and that of Cuchulainn, the heroic figure from the mythological past whom Yeats had brought to life in poem and play. Their noble and doomed act of defiance had much of the theatrical about it. The stage this time was history and the players, who in their individual lives embodied perhaps as many contradictions as Maud Gonne (Patrick Pearse himself, who read the Proclamation on the steps of the Post Office, was son to an English father), were caught up in an heroic gesture which, in Yeats' famous words, expressed the "terrible beauty" of a nation's destiny.

The compelling purity of such moments cannot, of course, be sustained. The years of guerilla warfare that the gesture of 1916 stimulated and the sad squalor of the Civil War which followed the Treaty with Great Britain in 1922 (which allowed 26 counties of Ireland something akin to Dominion status) forced that truth home. The service of Cathleen was a cruel one, her moods and whims treacherous. Yet in developing the arts of modern guerilla warfare in those years the Irish were not only bravely demonstrating to the world the power of ancestral feelings but offering an object lesson in the hard school of twentieth-century anti-imperial struggle—a lesson which was to be soundly learnt in many parts of the world.

When the dust had settled it was possible to see what the years of blood had effected. Ireland was partitioned into two administrative areas. In one, Northern Ireland, a local parliament exercising powers devolved from Westminster protected the political and social interests of the Protestant majority of six northern counties; in the other a new government slowly took control of a 26-county state in

Right *The ruthless Black and Tans, dressed in distinctive khaki coats and green trousers, search a GPO wagon in Dublin in 1920. The Black and Tans were a British auxiliary police force deployed in Ireland between July 1920 and July 1921 when Anglo-Irish relations were so strained that a large part of the Irish police force resigned.*

Left *Egerton Shelswell-White, owner of Bantry House, County Cork, in the Rose Room with its Gobelin tapestries. Built in 1771, Bantry House survived the Troubles, but maintenance is a never-ending problem.*

Below *Doneraile Court, County Cork, also built in the eighteenth century, is being restored by the Irish Georgian Society.*

Right *Dublin's famous Abbey Theatre, just off O'Connell Street, was founded by W.B. Yeats and Lady Gregory in 1904 to encourage Irish writers. The present-day building also houses the Peacock Theatre, where experimental work is put on.*

Below The Plough and the Stars *by Sean O'Casey caused riots when it was first performed at the Abbey Theatre in 1926. Audiences objected to O'Casey's unheroic treatment of the 1916 Rising.*

Far right, bottom *A sniper and lookouts in a Dublin street during the Civil War precipitated by the Anglo-Irish Treaty of 1921.*

which the great majority of citizens were in fact conservatively minded rural dwellers loyal to an austere and authoritarian Catholicism. A national revolution had taken place—the Union Jack no longer flew over Dublin Castle—but the social order in both parts of the island had not been radically disturbed. The new government in the Irish Free State, as it was known, essentially represented the interests of the landowners of rural Ireland, that class whose power had been asserted in the late nineteenth century and which had seized control of their farms from Anglo-Irish landlords through a series of Land Acts of the Westminster parliament.

It was Anglo-Ireland that was the principal victim of the national revolution. That once aggressively powerful social caste, identified by political support of the union with Great Britain, by Protestantism of the Anglican variety, by possession of vast tracts of the Irish soil and by patrician disdain for the mass of the Irish people, endured an eclipse as rapid and total in the early twentieth century as that of Tsarist Russia. Many of their sons perished in the Great War, many great families chose exile when it was clear that Irish independence was inevitable, and many of their big houses were razed to the ground in the fires of the War of Independence and the Civil War. Between 1921 and 1923 at least 192 such houses met this fate.

For Ireland the destruction of these houses was a real loss. For they contained many fine pictures, much good Irish furniture, and they had been designed and built by Irish craftsmen and workers. Only in recent years has modern Ireland begun to recognize this fact and sought to preserve those examples of Anglo-Ireland's architecture that escaped the fires of war and the effects of protracted neglect.

Below *The poet W.B. Yeats (1865-1939), Nobel laureate and Sligo's most famous son.*

Fortunately much of Anglo-Ireland's legacy to modern Ireland took less perishable form. For as their class lost its political and social power a number of enlightened and brilliantly creative individuals, associated in varying ways with Anglo-Ireland, committed themselves to the cultural renewal of their country. Douglas Hyde, son of a Church of Ireland clergyman and later to become Ireland's first President, helped to found the Gaelic League which strove energetically to revive the vernacular use of Ireland's ancient tongue. Lady Gregory of Coole in County Galway, with W.B. Yeats, established the Abbey Theatre, which in 1925 received a state subsidy from the new government (the first theater in the world to receive patronage of this kind); and in 1923 Yeats himself brought honor on the new state, of whose parliament he was a Senator, when he received the Nobel Prize for Literature. The poet's sure esthetic sense, indeed, made itself felt in the very practical matter of money. He served on the committee which decided upon the quite beautiful designs for an Irish coinage.

Distinctive Anglo-Irish institutions survived in the new state—the Royal Irish Academy (with its traditions of learning and scholarship), Trinity College, Dublin (one of the oldest universities in the English-speaking world), and the Royal Dublin Society, which at its annual Horse Show in the capital allowed a new political and social élite to mix with their former masters in an atmosphere of relaxed style and shared enthusiasm for thoroughbred horse flesh. Anglo-Ireland's experience in this century of bitter anti-colonialism was markedly fortunate—the fact that Dublin's two cathedrals remain to this day centers of Anglican worship reflects a profound tolerance at the heart of Irish life. But something of Anglo-Ireland's sense of social disintegration and loss was expressed in the work of Ireland's other Nobel laureate, Samuel Beckett, who made his own anguished response to a Protestant upbringing in a stiflingly genteel Dublin suburb of the 1920s a metaphor for the spiritual dislocation of modern man.

The new state was not all tolerance, however. An Irish identity had to be forged and protected. The Irish language was to be revived

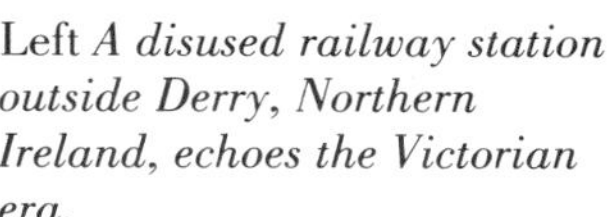

Left *A disused railway station outside Derry, Northern Ireland, echoes the Victorian era.*

Left *Herding cows along a road in Connemara.*

Far left *Sheep can be found wandering all over the unfenced landscape.*

LEIGH'S
RICE KRISPIES
RICE KRISPIES

and Catholic values imposed in crucial areas of personal morality (divorce, for example, was forbidden). A rigorous censorship of literature was established in 1929 which for almost four decades was to ban works by almost every twentieth-century writer of note. Church and state seemed united in a crusade to maintain a *cordon sanitaire* around the country. A conservative people was governed by conservative politicians who deferred to priest and prelate. Of priests there was no shortage. Religion was a growth industry flourishing alone in a society where droves of young people emigrated each year from a country in which they could find no livelihood. And they left to a chorus of ecclesiastical warnings on the temptations they would face in pagan England, America and Australia and with denunciations of the dangers of sexual licence ringing in their ears. Reasons for the extraordinary puritanism of newly independent Ireland are not hard to find: the economic rigors of life on the small farms throughout the country enforced sexual abstinence where a premarital pregnancy could be ruinous; an insecure nationalism encouraged zealous excess, an isolationism of manners and morals. But it is hard not to sense something older and more rooted in perennial aspects of the Irish psyche which links modern pilgrimages still undertaken by large numbers

Far left *A brightly painted shop front, complete with thatched roof, in 'the Grocers' Republic.'*

Below *A pub in Kinvara, County Galway.*

Left *Eamon de Valera at the center of proceedings during his inauguration as President of the Republic in 1959. He remained in office until 1973.*

Above *In an Irish pub, any time is Guinness time.*

of people to such holy sites as Lough Derg and Croagh Patrick with the ancient ascetism of Celtic Christianity.

From 1932 onwards (with brief interruptions) the austere, distinctly clerical Eamon de Valera presided over this inward-looking society of cautious shopkeepers, farmers and small businessmen, a society one disenchanted writer bitterly satirized as "the Grocers' Republic." De Valera aspired to Irish self-sufficiency. Neutrality in World War II was an expression of his dedication to the absolute of national independence. What he wanted for his people was, as he told them on St. Patrick's Day in 1943, an Ireland "... which we dreamed ...would be the home of a people who valued material wealth only as a basis of right living, of a people who were satisfied with frugal comfort and devoted their leisure to the things of the spirit; a land whose countryside would be bright with cosy homesteads, whose fields and villages would be joyous with sounds of industry, the romping of sturdy children, the contests of athletic youths, the laughter of comely maidens; whose firesides would be the forums of the wisdom of serene old age."

Such a romantic view of Irish life, though commendable for its idealism, took little account of the desperate poverty of much of rural and urban Ireland, of an emigration that was draining the country of its energetic young and of the human waste which an angry, eloquent Patrick Kavanagh exposed in his terrifying long poem of 1941, *The Great Hunger*. Kavanagh's work was indeed an indictment of a political and social order that delivered to so many only a living death. Cathleen Ni Houlihan had surrendered to a possessive widowed mother who demanded no sacrifice of her sons on the altar of patriotism; she sought from them rather the lifelong self-abnegation of sexual abstinence.

The Irish Free State was founded in 1922. The same year James Joyce published his major novel, *Ulysses*. The Free State seemed dedicated to an image of Ireland as uniquely pious and self-sufficient. Joyce's great book, immortalizing Dublin as few other novels have

Left *The puck sits beneath the Republican Tricolor during the Annual Puck Fair in Killorglin, County Kerry. The flag on the right is that of the province of Ulster.*

done for any other place, revealed by contrast that Irish people were much the same as people the world over. Rich in local, distinguishing characteristics of wit, love of myth, gossip and song, they nevertheless share with most of humanity a taste for the drink and normally various sexual needs. Molly Bloom, whose ripe soliloquy concludes the book, is no better than she should be, and all the better for that, as representative of Irish womanhood. She gave the lie to all who wanted to pretend that the Ireland of Cathleen Ni Houlihan and the possessive mother was the only Ireland.

By the 1950s Ireland's economic and social problems had become acute. The quest for self-sufficiency was obviously futile in a decade when emigration and unemployment were putting in question the very existence of the state. It was time for a new departure. Under the energetic leadership of a new prime minister, Sean Lemass, Ireland took the decision to abandon economic isolation, to open its economy to large-scale foreign investment. Sights were now set on membership of the European Community and on the consumer society. It was time to abandon dreams of a

Left *A traditional cottage in County Donegal.*

Below *A bungalow at Ballybunion, County Kerry, complete with trompe l'oeil wall.*

glorious past and to unleash some youthful energy. The people responded with a will. Change was the tonic. From Saskatoon to Sidney the 1960s quickened rhythms and the pace of things. Ireland was eager to join the dance. The Second Vatican Council had given Irish Catholicism a less intimidating face. The national television station which began broadcasting in 1962 opened the air waves to vigorous debates on traditional values. Hemlines went up, inhibitions down. Fortunes were made.

In 20 years the young Republic (formally declared in 1949) underwent a social transformation. Emigration ceased almost completely and the population, which had declined inexorably since the famine of the 1840s, began to climb (it now stands at 3.25 million). A society that had been marked by a preponderance of elderly and unmarried people became unique in Western Europe for the youthfulness and fertility of its citizenry. By the end of the 1970s over half the population was under 25 years of age. Education, not religion, was now the boom industry, giving contemporary Ireland one of the best educated populations in the world.

In the 1960s and 1970s Ireland changed

Below *The recently completed Financial Services Centre in Dublin testifies to a new, outward-looking spirit of enterprise in the Republic.*

from a rural to an urban society. Dublin's population grew to over 1 million, while the flight from the small farms of rural Ireland left much of the countryside in the hands of new-style entrepreneurial farmers who exploited the agricultural policies of the EEC (Ireland entered in 1973) to remarkable effect. A landscape that had scarcely changed since the nineteenth century in the 1970s produced a crop of luxurious bungalows, banishing the traditional cottage to the tourist brochure and the exile's dream.

The strain on the burgeoning cities was enormous, Dublin particularly bearing the brunt. Huge new housing estates sprang up where many thousands of young families, many of them recently uprooted from the land, tried to cope with the demands of urban life. Often basic services were neglected in these new wastelands and "alienation" entered the vocabulary of Irish ills. But foreign holidays were cheap, the Costa del Sol a yearly parole from commuter bus and supermarket queue. And things were getting better. Weren't they?

Well, yes and no. Certainly there was a genuine rise in living standards (between 1957 and 1980 there was an 80 percent rise in personal consumption per head in real terms and

Below *The pretty harbour of Cobh, County Cork, dominated by its neo-Gothic cathedral, was a major departure point for steamers carrying emigrants to America. The port is still used by a substantial fishing fleet.*

Right *Ian Paisley addressing a Loyalist rally in Belfast. The slogan 'No Surrender' survives from the Siege of Derry.*

Above *The presence of the British Army in Northern Ireland is reassuring to some and a provocation to others.*

disposable personal income in real terms doubled in the same period). But such statistics disguise what studies of Irish poverty in the 1970s suggested: that at least a quarter of the population and perhaps one third lived below a "poverty line" estimated on the basis of social security levels of payment. And the burden of foreign debt increased rapidly in the same decade to provoke serious economic crisis in the 1980s. And there was the appalling, threatening problem of the North.

Since 1922 all Irish governments had been dedicated to the anti-Partition cause. The Border was a wound inflicted on the Irish nation by the duplicitous Lloyd George. Only its removal would end the old quarrel with England. The fact that a million Protestant Unionists were implacably opposed to incorporation in an all-Ireland state was to a very great extent simply ignored. It was naively assumed that when the British decided to leave Ireland the Unionists would come to their senses and throw in their lot with the island's majority. In expectation of that utopian outcome, for 40 years nothing much was done to make reunification any kind a practical possibility. Indeed a state intent on enshrining Catholic social policy in its legislation and Constitution and on emphasizing the Gaelic traditions of its people might well be considered to have consolidated Partition. Furthermore a state which could not provide its own population with a decent standard of living could hardly lay serious claims on an economically better-placed population in a neighboring jurisdiction. It was Sean Lemass, a practical visionary, who saw that reunification could only occur when the Republic had achieved sufficient economic power to make it possible and that in the meantime the two parts of Ireland should co-operate

Below *The Women's Peace Movement was started by Betty Williams and Mairead Corrigan in response to years of violence in Northern Ireland. Both women were awarded the Nobel Peace Prize in 1976.*

to their mutual advantage. On an historic day in January 1965 Lemass visited the Prime Minister of Northern Ireland at the Stormont Parliament Buildings in Belfast. Perhaps North and South could, in pursuit of realistic aims, break the log jam of decades of suspicion and prejudice and in eventual EEC membership make the border an anachronistic irrelevance. It was not to be.

Terence O'Neill, the Northern Irish Prime Minister, announced in 1964 that he intended "to make Northern Ireland prosperous and to build bridges between the two traditions in our community." This and his meeting with Lemass and a later visit to Dublin itself were too much for some of his Northern Irish enemies. The ambitious, demagogic Ian Paisley exploited fears of a sellout by O'Neill to revive old sectarian passions upon whose back he hoped to rise to power. There could be no accommodation with Irish nationalism nor any compromise with the Catholic nationalist minority in the Northern state. They had never accepted the validity of Partition and treacherously withheld loyalty from Queen and country. Such was Paisley's poisonous message. No surrender.

The Catholic minority in Northern Ireland had endured four decades of second-class citizenship and discrimination. A new generation of educated young people in its midst, which had seized the educational opportunities afforded by the British welfare state, was quite unprepared to accept that Northern Catholics should continue to be so abused by the resented majority. The civil rights movement was born, bred of the radicalism of young people everywhere in the 1960s and of a profound sense of social and national grievance. Reaction from the majority was swift and bloody. Civil disruption quickly went beyond the control of the local forces of law and order and the British Army was dispatched by the British government to restore and maintain the peace. And there it has remained since 1969, through

Below *A Loyalist mural in County Derry depicting the victory of 'King Billy,' William of Orange, at the Battle of the Boyne in 1690.*

Left *A bird's eye view of industrial Belfast. One third of the population of Northern Ireland lives in Belfast.*

Below *A Sinn Féin mural on the Falls Road in west Belfast spells out hopes for the future.*

two decades of violence that have made Belfast and Derry one with Saigon, Tehran and Beirut and an object of sporadic attention by the international media.

In the 1960s the Irish Republican Army (IRA) seemed a defeated force. This small group of guerillas (illegal in both parts of Ireland), dedicated to Irish unity and to the removal of the Border, called off a military campaign in 1962 when failure stared it in the face. In the era of O'Neill and Lemass, of consumerism and ecumenism, it seemed irrelevant, part of the past. But the civil disturbances of the late 1960s in Northern Ireland, and the presence on the streets in Derry and Belfast of the old enemy, the British Army, once more gave the guerilla a sea in which to swim. Nurtured in the Catholic ghetto's fear of sectarian attack and anger at the heavy-handed excesses of the British soldiery, the provisional IRA emerged in the early 1970s as a well-organized, determined guerilla army which has sustained its campaign in Northern Ireland and Britain ever since.

Above *Belfast has some of the largest dock cranes in the world. In the nineteenth century shipbuilding and linen were the city's two great industries. Today the linen industry has disappeared and shipbuilding is in a state of collapse, despite massive subsidies from Britain and the EEC.*

In comparison with guerilla wars in other parts of the world "the troubles" in the North may seem tame. In many areas of the province life has continued almost normally. The IRA exercises, despite the propaganda, a certain restraint, as does the British Army. Horrific atrocities have been committed by all sides, but periods of comparative peace allow the underlying problems of the area to seem less in need of immediate attention than they really are. The IRA and the British Army have each achieved a kind of stalemate in which neither can defeat the other. Life goes on. So does the war.

But Northern Ireland is a small place, about the size of Yorkshire. Its population of 1.5 million lives mostly in the Belfast and Derry areas where the violence has been most spectacular. So war has become an intimate part of the people's consciousness. Everyone knows someone who has been killed or injured. A weirdly local, almost domestic war is how ordinary people experience it. Gelignite mixed in with the soup spoons. Blood on the kitchen floor. And an entire generation has grown up in the ghettoes for whom checkpoints, summary arrest and interrogation, and the sniper's bullet are taken for normality.

Reactions in the South to the Northern trauma have been various. A small minority has given active support and encouragement to the IRA, providing safe houses to men on the run, passing on information. An indeterminate though probably not large section of the population gives tacit support to the movement while regretting some of its methods. Most people just hope "the troubles" can be contained north of the Border and try to ignore them. On two occasions it seemed that would

be impossible. In 1972, following Bloody Sunday in Derry when British paratroopers shot dead 13 unarmed civil rights marchers, a wave of popular revulsion led to the burning of the British Embassy in Dublin and to a sense that national honor might demand even greater retribution. Almost ten years later the deaths of ten republican hunger strikers in a Northern jail revived atavistic feelings that threatened to overwhelm the official moderation which has governed the Irish state's response to the Northern crisis throughout. At these moments it was as if Cathleen Ni Houlihan was once again challenging the nation with her message of blood and sacrifice.

Left *The funeral of Provisional IRA hunger striker Joseph McDonnell in 1981. The gunmen are masked and the coffin is draped with the Irish Tricolor. Many hunger strikes were staged by 'Provo' prisoners in Northern Ireland in the early 1980s in an attempt to gain recognition as political prisoners.*

Two things may account for the fact that this message now lacks its former mesmeric power. Nightly television reports have brought home to most people the sheer ghastliness of modern terrorist violence, the difference, in the dramatist John Synge's words, between "a gallous story" and "a dirty deed." And a taste of prosperity made many disinclined to exchange a recently achieved well-being for the rigors of a war of national liberation. And in the 1980s that novel Irish experience of economic success began to seem a temporary alleviation of the more authentic Irish condition of poverty. In times of great economic insecurity, therefore, few possessed much interest in further rocking the ship of state in the turbulent waters of national revolution.

Britain and Ireland have also realized that their national interests coalesce in sustaining some measure of stability in Northern Ireland. In 1985, despite strenuous objections from Unionists in the North, the two governments signed the Anglo-Irish Agreement which gave the government of the Republic of Ireland a degree of control in the northern part of the island. This agreement effectively established a surreptitious form of joint authority over the province which has proved markedly durable, even though the violence it was expected to diminish has continued unabated. Current attempts to involve the Unionists in the complex negotiations that might restore a legislative chamber to the North (the Unionist-controlled parliament of Stormont was abolished by the British government in 1972) have so far proved fruitless.

In the 1980s the Irish economy, after two decades of apparent health, exhibited symptoms of serious, possibly even life-threatening, malaise. The worldwide recession bit deep in Ireland. Foreign indebtedness rose frighteningly. Taxation increased so steeply that the ordinary Irish worker had the dubious distinction of being the poorest supertax payer in the world. The agricultural sector, after ten years of expansion and profit, was faced with problems of over-production in the European Community and by challenges to the Common

Right *The imposing exterior of Government Buildings in Dublin. Originally built to house the Royal College of Science in 1911, they became the administrative center of government in 1922. Government Buildings stand beside Leinster House, once the town house of the Duke of Leinster and now the seat of Ireland's parliament.*

Below *Irish taoiseach Charles Haughey poses in front of the flags of the EEC. Presidency of the Council of the European Community changes every six months. In 1990 it was the turn of the Republic of Ireland.*

Left *A John F. Kennedy tapestry in Krugers Bar, Dunquin, County Kerry. Of Irish descent, JFK was also America's first Roman Catholic president.*

Agricultural Policy from which Irish farmers had so significantly benefitted. Crime rates in the cities rose dramatically. Vandalism and drug-trafficking became endemic. The black economy burgeoned as harrassed breadwinners sought to augment inadequate incomes. Emigration once again became the safety valve of a social crisis that otherwise might have boiled over in turmoil on the streets. Many thousands of young Irish men and women left the country, many for Britain, others for Boston and New York. The fortunate left with a university degree and a Green Card which gave them legal status in the United States. Thousands left with neither and now exist perilously outside the law in traditional Irish occupations in North America, as building workers, bar staff and domestic servants, afraid to return to Ireland for holidays lest they be denied re-entry by the vigilant U.S. immigration authorities.

In 1987 the Irish government set about reforming public services in a belated and desperate attempt to check the inevitable drift to national bankruptcy. Savage cuts were made in such areas as education and health (despite explicit pre-election assertions by the winning party that these were entirely unnecessary). For the last four years the country has been in an effective state of semi-consciousness, weak from the surgery that has been applied, unsure of recovery and fearful of further nasty medicine. The public has accepted, as a seriously ill patient will, bland assurances that all is well, that the economy is in stronger shape, despite manifest evidence to the contrary. Unemployment creeps towards 300,000 in a country of just over 3 million people. Huge gaps in lifestyle and expectation have opened up between the ostentatiously wealthy and the immiserated poor. The young leave in droves. Government increasingly becomes a matter of photo-calls, style, hype and public relations combining to suggest delusions of grandeur as the edifice of state shudders. Scandal in the private sector becomes commonplace in a commercial culture where the stroke, the shady deal and the offshore tax haven are deemed normal business practice.

There are signs, however, that the condition is not terminal. Artistic life, despite the economic and moral crisis, remains a focus of much energy. It is striking how many gifted young Irish men and women are currently making their mark in the worlds of popular music, cinema and fashion, while the international publishers in London and New York still include in their lists remarkably high proportions of emerging Irish literary talent. The sustained achievements of the country's older writers and artists remain a source of great pride to many, an assurance in difficult times of national excellence. Seamus Heaney is Professor of Poetry in Oxford University. Brien Friel's play *Dancing at Lughnasa* was a major success in London and on Broadway. The annual Booker Prize shortlist almost always includes an Irish entry; a recent one was John McGahern's novel *Amongst Women*, a telling study of female repression and power. That it appeared in 1989, the same year as Friel's stage success, with its joyous celebration of female life energies, may suggest that Cathleen Ni Houlihan, an old harridan for all her momentary beauty, with her calls for male blood sacrifice, has at last been superseded in contemporary Ireland by demands for the empowerment of women in the real, not the mythological, social order. As if to confirm this

Below *A wildlife sanctuary near Courtmacsherry, County Cork. Courtmacsherry is a quiet resort on the Seven Heads Peninsula, popular with sea anglers.*

impression, in 1990 the Irish electorate took the chance to reject at the polls the presidential candidate of the ruling party (naturally a man) and to elect as President of Ireland a woman lawyer who throughout her career has been a notable defender of women's rights. At the end of a decade in which economic insecurity allowed conservative forces to enshrine and reinforce traditional Catholic values in the Irish Constitution (two referenda proscribed abortion under any circumstances and re-affirmed the proscription on divorce), President Mary Robinson's election suggests that Irish society has not become entirely supine in the face of repeated blows and that women especially (her election was greatly affected by the women's vote) have not accepted the dismal status quo.

Right *Rosaries and devotional pictures decorate many Catholic homes.*

Mother Church 5

Brendan Kennelly

In Ireland you often hear the phrase "Ninety-six percent of the people of the Republic are Catholics." An entire history of pride in survival is contained in that phrase. In the south of Ireland this statistical dominance finds social expression in ways both obvious and subtle. In the north of Ireland, where Protestants are in the majority, we hear a good deal of talk about discrimination against Catholics in the workplace. It's a topsy-turvy situation; but I would say that the southern Protestant *feels* more secure in his political situation than his more powerful co-religionist does in the north. Common to all sections of the religious community, however, is the problem of identity. It is a problem that seems to deepen with the passing of time.

For many reasons, most of them historical, Irish Catholicism is almost obsessively concerned with its own identity. An Irish Catholic is not always easily identifiable as a Christian. Ireland is full of Catholics who are not at all sure about the use of this term "Christian." There's something vaguely Protestant about it. But this is finally beginning to change. A new generation of young men and women is growing up which is not too concerned with labels, which insists on thinking things out for itself. This insistence is part of the very real strength of the new Ireland.

When I was a boy at school we were told that it wasn't right to think things out for yourself. You had to be obedient, to accept the Church's word on practically everything. Thinking things out for yourself could mean that you'd "become a freethinker" and so be in danger of hell's fire. That was the irony: hell was where you were free to think as you wished.

Below *Open-air Mass in Drogheda during the Pope's visit to Ireland in 1979.*

We had regular examinations in Religious Knowledge. The Council of Trent, the Infallibility of the Pope, the Albigensian Heresy, and so on. For about six or seven weeks each year we studied nothing all day but this vast, celestial and infernal topic called Religious Knowledge. We ate, drank, slept and dreamed it. We argued about it before and after football games. We asked questions of adults about matters like the Virgin Birth, the nature of venial and mortal sin, consanguinity, affinity, and what we'd all look like on the morning of the Resurrection. Most of us, who'd rarely spent much time out of our native villages, chatted casually but constantly about Calvin and Luther and Garibaldi and Cavour and more Popes than I have space to mention here. And all the time it was driven into us how specially privileged we were to belong to the One, True, Holy, Catholic and Apostolic Church. Often, when we were playing football in a muddy field and I saw my mates Scratcher Roche, Turkey Murphy, Barabbas Kelly, The Bishop Tracey, The Scourge Callaghan, Threeballs Connor and Biscuits Bambury up to their noses in muck, their togs in filthy shreds, their faces black masks of jubilation, I wondered would they look like this on the morning of the Resurrection, and weren't they now, each one of them a member of the One True Church, in such a mucky state their own mothers would be hard put to recognize them? And if your mother didn't recognize you, who in God's name could?

This religious knowledge got into our blood, bones, brains and hearts. Did not some Jesuit say: "Give me a boy before he's seven, and he's mine for life?" I know exactly what the man meant. In Ireland religion is a systematic assault on individual and collective consciousness. It is not sporadic, it is constant, organized, permanent. It is a kind of spiritual imperialism. It infiltrates and in many respects dominates your ways of thinking and feeling. It

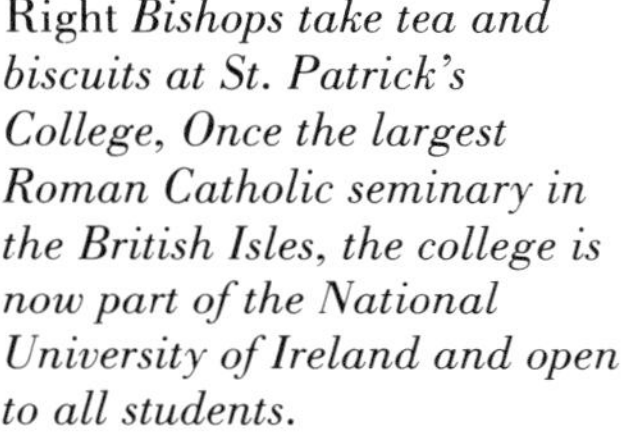

Right *Bishops take tea and biscuits at St. Patrick's College, Once the largest Roman Catholic seminary in the British Isles, the college is now part of the National University of Ireland and open to all students.*

Left *Grandmother and granddaughter watch the ferry come in at Inishmore, Aran Islands.*

Above *A rustic shrine to the Virgin Mary. Wife, mother and faithful follower, Mary is still promoted as a role model for Irish women.*

is insinuating, forceful, pervasive, terminal. It has many attractive elements. It does a fair amount of good. And until recently, when people for many reasons grew more and more independent of their priests, it did a fair amount of damage. You cannot really flirt with Catholicism. It's either a love affair or a hate affair, despite the routine, almost mechanical nature of its practice in Ireland. Either way, it invades the soul, takes comprehensive possession of it. Catholicism is dramatic and ritualistic, beyond mere intellect and reason. In its Irish form, at any rate, it's a blood and guts religion with a wholly unapologetic mystical content. People often think they can shake it off. They cannot. Not completely, anyway.

"What sort of atheist are you?" one non-believer said to another.

"A Catholic atheist" was the reply.

Irish Catholicism is often said to be mindless; and there's a truth in this. There is not a strong tradition of individual thinking among Irish theologians, although the work of priests such as Enda MacDonagh, Patrick Hederman, Donal Dorr and Dermot Lane is the product of strong, independent minds. But the *tradition* is not like this. The tradition is profoundly conservative and cautious. It is anti-intellectual but mentally agile.

Over the past few years, continuing the tradition of independence mentioned above, there are signs of new, fresh thinking among some of the younger priests, and also among the younger nuns. There is, above all, an increasing awareness of the nature and consequences of the appalling problems of emigration and unemployment. Nuns like Sister Stanislaus Kennedy, a truly heroic woman, and priests like Father Peter McVerry do tremendous work among the Dublin poor. The real strength of the Irish Church lies in its gritty pastoral character; and when it turns its attention to social problems such as unemployment, crime, drug addiction, alcoholism and various forms of sexual abuse, it is capable of work that is as magnificent as it is anonymous.

There's a real difference between Irish Catholicism and Roman Catholicism. This is so, I believe, because Ireland is an island, its landscape one of remarkable variety, a beautiful, green island washed by seas of prejudice, an island careful to guard its own ways of looking at life and love, politics and hate and sex, jealously protecting its own inherited values, distrustful of new ones. Today, there is much talk of "links with Europe" and the deliberate "Europeanization of Ireland." And this process *is* taking place. But never forget that Ireland is an island, and the Irish are an island people. They are not always conscious of this fact, yet their everyday talk is full of the assumptions and attitudes of a deeply rooted insularity. Insularity should not be confused with provincialism; the provincial is basically distrustful of his own inheritance and has a policy of apeing what he thinks is of more value and in better taste. The provincial is likely to end up being an imitative nobody, a severed shell of a man or woman, a sort of sophisticated slave. The island person, on the other hand, has his own world, his own tested codes and beliefs, his own proven ways. This doesn't mean that he's not open to change; it *does* mean that you have to work very hard to get him to begin to change his mind about what matters to him. He *knows* what matters to him.

The Irish are a sticky, rooted lot. Although they wander all over the world, although they emigrate in their reluctant thousands and are scattered to the four quarters of the earth, the Irish are a sticky lot.

Most of them stick to Irish ways with a tenacity that many a European might find incredible.

In Ireland, history is a glue. It glues an Irishman to his ways of thinking. And his insularity gives further strength to that glue.

"Thank God we're surrounded by water" is the refrain of a song written and sung by Dominic Behan, Brendan's brother. Dominic may have intended this to be ironic, but the line, taken on its own, is a celebration acceptable to many. Rise up there, Dominic, and sing it again! Why did your mother put shoes on you? "Thank God we're surrounded by water." Thank God indeed.

Above *A fishing boat being blessed to ensure good fishing and safety at sea.*

Is it not easy, given this deeply rooted insularity, to see why some people find Ireland "quaint," "charming," "a delightful place to visit" (Brendan Behan used to say that Ireland was a lovely place to get a postcard from!) These words and phrases are merely ways of refusing to get to grips with the dark entanglements, the extremely complex phenomenon of insularity, the nature of its self-sufficiency, its subtle and surprising openness, that state of

Above *Installation of Brendan Comiskey as Bishop of Ferns at St. Aidan's Cathedral, Enniscorthy, County Wexford.*

Right *Nuns mingle with shoppers in O'Connell Street, Dublin. Skirts rather than floor-length habits are a fairly recent phenomenon.*

egotistical, vigilant isolation in which almost anything can happen.

Out of Ireland have we come.
Great hatred, little room
Maimed us at the start.
I carry from my mother's womb
A fanatic heart.

Great hatred, little room. Congested tensions. Incestuous horrors. Isolated fanaticism. Blind lives. Unthinking hatreds. Hovering betrayals. Unbreakable loyalties. No surrender. To hell or to Connaught. To hell with the Pope. To hell with King William. A land of severed intensity. A land of mindless, savage slogans and murderous cliches. Pleasant, decent people riddled with prejudice; even in the exercise of their truly delightful humor, it will amaze you to witness it once you come in contact with it, if you listen to the language behind the laughter. (Ah! but do you recognize your own buried prejudices, dearest reader? Do I recognize mine? I am quite sure this article is full of prejudices that I cannot even recognize. Of that at least I am sure. And that is the very nature of prejudice; one is so full of it one cannot even see it. Yet let me not be intimidated by this recognition!)

The Irish Catholic Church is full, as I am, of this kind of buried prejudice. The nuns, on the

Above *Two kinds of solace for the soul.*

whole, have no real power in the Church. Why don't they stand up for themselves the way Sister Stanislaus Kennedy ("Sister Stan" to thousands of admiring Dubliners) does? The bishops and priests rule the holy roost. They want it that way. They smile and dominate, dominate and smile. They cut out the women. The Irish Church is sexless. It doesn't know how to handle sex. Or maybe it knows too well. It cuts it out of life, or tries to. Yet even as I write this, I realize that the new young Catholics of Ireland, this new outward-looking, Europeanized generation is frequently very much at odds with the teachings of the Church on sexual matters. It may seem incredible to people from other countries, but the sale of condoms to youngsters, and the outrage which this causes in some quarters, still provides the headlines in our leading national newspapers. In this autumn of 1991 unemployment is at its highest in the history of the state, the country faces the grim statistic of nearly one in every five being out of work—and the sale of condoms can still provoke a very heated nationwide discussion. More of a dogfight than a discussion, in fact. And all it proves is our relentless moral juvenility.

Sometimes I think that the Irish concern with sex, and more particularly the Irish bishops' pronouncements about sex, exist to take our

Right *Pilgrims climb to the top of Croagh Patrick, County Mayo, on Garland Sunday, the last Sunday in July. Many go barefoot. At the top autographed pictures of the Saint are on sale!*

minds off the real problems afflicting our society. The bishops say it is all right to *be* sexual. But please don't *do* it. Part of the deepest problem facing the Irish Catholic Church is this inability to handle the problems of being *and* doing. The trouble is that instead of trying to reconcile them, the Church tends to separate them.

Here is an extract from the Irish bishops' Pastoral, *Love Is For Life*, 1985 (Popular Edition): "The true meaning of sexuality is also negated in homosexual acts and sexual relations between homosexuals. We must distinguish homosexual orientation from homosexual acts. Objectively, homosexual acts are intrinsically and gravely immoral. Homosexual tendencies, however, as distinct from homosexual actions, can be innate and irreversible. They can cause drives and temptations which are difficult to control or resist. For such persons, some homosexual actions may well lack the full freedom and deliberateness necessary to constitute grave sin. Each case must be judged individually and compassionately."

Two things strike me about this extract. There is, first, the situation in which a group of celibates tells other grown men how to behave with each other. It's as if a non-drinker advised a drinker on the nature and effects of whiskey. Do these bishops really know what they're talking about? Or are they sincerely talking out of some lofty theory of sexuality? Secondly, there is a genuine current of compassionate understanding in the writing. It's a strange and characteristic piece of writing, a blend of brutal readiness to pronounce on what's right and wrong and a genuine thrust toward compassionate understanding. This second element is the element that needs to be strengthened and

Left *Another of Ireland's many shrines to the Holy Virgin. This one is sited at the foot of the Paps at Gortnagone, County Kerry.*

Above *A mother comforts her son. Despite their slowly changing status, Irish women are still most numerous in the 'caring' professions – social work, nursing, teaching.*

Right *Marriage is still seen as the ideal state for Irish men and women. Every year, in September, thousands of single people in search of a partner flock to Lisdoonvarna, County Clare, for the month-long Festival of Bachelors. Does true love await this newly-met couple? Ireland is unique among the countries of Europe in having no civil divorce.*

developed. People have difficulties enough in their attempts to relate to each other, both in bed and out of it, without a bunch of middle-aged celibates telling them exactly how to do it, or how not to do it; but many people need plenty of that compassionate understanding which is also present in the Pastoral.

The main trouble with any gathering of bishops is that they tend inevitably to become sternly and collectively judgemental. Irish bishops should bring thoughtful nuns or just a selection of ordinary, intelligent, sensitive women along to their meetings. These women would soon take the shine off the bishops' bliss, soften their hard judgemental maleness, deepen their compassion and diminish their pomposity. The Irish Church needs to be deliberately and comprehensively feminized. The problem with bishops is that they're more interested in telling you what is wrong than what is right, more interested in respectability than in respect, more determined to exclude women than to allow them to contribute. Bishops wear too many gorgeous clothes on their minds as well as on their bodies. They should learn to walk naked now and then. If they did, they'd be more lively and less pompous. Perhaps many of these men are not really pompous at all, but they give the impression of being so.

How close are these bishops to the people they claim to represent, to the people they *do*, in fact, represent? Not very close, I'd say. These strong, intelligent, potentially compassionate, respectable bishopmen are apparently more interested in power than in love. Power, in my experience, does not always corrupt; it certainly doesn't *necessarily* corrupt. But power does tend to make people boring. I notice that a lot of powerful people like nodding their heads "wisely" during a talk or chat. This is meant to exonerate them from the risks, hazards and follies of an animated Irish conversation. Bishops tend to be head-nodders. It's boring. These "wise" nodding heads do a lot to outlaw sexual expression; except, of course, in marriage.

Marriage. I asked two Irishwomen, "What is marriage?" The first answered, "Tryin' not to hate the man you believe you love." The second said, "It's a woman sharin' problems and troubles with a man so that she won't feel too alone." There is more wisdom in one harrassed woman than in a thousand pampered bishops. The more people know about marriage, the less exalted and highfalutin' their statements about it tend to be. But Irish bishops know all about marriage; that's why they pronounce so majestically on the matter. And that's why they never get married. Cute boyos. Stay single and celibate and advise the lads and lassies about sex.

Frequently in Ireland marriage is the taming of sex. It domesticates the excitement out of sex. Marriage is children, that is (in the Church's eyes) the continuity and expansion of the Church. Marriage is harnessing wild energies. Marriage, above all, is settling a man and a woman down. Let them grow for a while, then settle them down. When I think of these two single words, "settle down," a thousand stories, grave and merry stories of courtship and marriage, rise in my head. Settle down. Like a corpse in a coffin. But don't forget about the Resurrection!

It is important to grasp this idea of the implacable maleness of the Irish Church. Without it, you will not understand how women are used even as they are raised on pedestals. One of the most effective ways to get rid of a woman is to put her on a pedestal. The notion of a Miss World is an exercise in this sort of lofty degradation. The Irish Mother, as created by the male Irish Church, is a sort of claustrophobic domestic equivalent of Miss World. Spectacularly elected, at once vaguely and prominently ludicrous, yet worth adoring. Take your prize, and vanish!

But again, here, things are changing. While that outmoded concept of motherhood still fairly widely prevails, many young Irishwomen of today are quick and passionate in their assertion of separateness from this pallid, domesticated maternal image. These new young women think like their counterparts in Britain, in Europe, in America, all through the world.

But the Church has always been keen to harness and direct female sexuality. If a man can do this, he will guarantee his own powerful position.

Spiritual tyranny or dominance is a subtle

thing. It wears many masks, ranging from the calmly benevolent to the furiously rhetorical to the sweetly coaxing to the violently blustering. The first thing I would say about it is that it usually works. And often the people who defend it most vigorously are its most obvious victims. That is why the "Irish Mother" of song and story, of legend and recitation, the bearer of infinite children, the begetter and defender of virtue, the heroine of countless ballads, is the first person to come to the defense of the Church's sexual policies, many of which would use women without mercy. Have more children or be damned. You are the home-builder, you must never leave the home. Obey your husband or go to hell. Conceive again, conceive again, conceive again. Such was the "advice" given to many women by priests not so very long ago. Get a woman to "obey" till "death do you part" and you have her not only for wife but for life. Make her a mother quickly, often, and forever.

Even in their extraordinarily limiting familial situations some women nevertheless became very powerful figures as mothers. But this demanded an unusually resourceful and shrewd personality. The majority of women were relatively powerless, frequently confined to the home for the greater part of their lives. An Englishman's home is said to be his castle; it was often an Irish mother's political arena. Some women achieved power there; the majority did not.

Many Irish writers have tried to get to grips with the gentle tyranny of motherhood. Indeed it is almost obligatory on Irish writers to grapple with this phenomenon. Mother. Mother Ireland. Mother Church. Mother whatever you will. In the following poem, I present a man who breaks free from the mothering-smothering forces in Irish society. When I read the poem on Irish Radio some years ago there were many indignant protests from Irish mothers. The plain fact is that I have the deepest admiration for these Irishwomen who work so hard to keep home and family together through good times and bad, sometimes despite the worst efforts of feckless and irresponsible husbands. But needless to say this admiration doesn't prevent me from saying what I have to say on the matter of emotional strangulation and freedom. The

Right *A well-manicured churchyard in Kilkenny.*

Above *Decorations like these can be seen on many graves in Ireland.*

poem is called *Moloney Up And At It.*

My soul from hell, the night the ould wan died,
Moloney said, I cried an' cried
Tears down. I'd been tied to her string
Through rack and hardship and the wild fling
O' youth, through manhood and the grey
Days when youth begins to slip away,
And now my addled heart and head
Were bound by the memory of the dead.

Well, anyway, after puttin' herself down
In the box, I went to the town
O' Lishtowel for a few drinks, and there
I met a Knockanore woman with red hair
And gamey eye. I made bold
And in a short time had told
Her my story. She cocked her ear and listened well.
We drank until the darkness fell
And for hours after. The talk
Spun on love. 'Can I walk
A piece with you?' says I. 'Moloney,' says she,
'You're welcome to do what you like with me.'
Fair enough! We left Lishtowel and struck the road,
Footin' it free over pothole
And gravel. The Knockanore woman was full o' guff
And harped on all the tricks o' love.
I upped with my question. She
Was willin' and free.

'Where would you like it?' says I. 'Well,' she said,
'God's green earth is a warm bed.'
'Right you are, girl,' says I.
It happened we were passin' by
Gale graveyard where my mother lay.
'What would you say
To this place?' says I. 'Moloney,' says she,
'If it's right with you, it's right with me.'

Straightaway, I opened the gate and led
The Knockanore woman over the dead
O' seven parishes. Talk of a flyer!
Fasht as they come an' hot as fire!
She fell down on the soft clay
Of a fresh grave, and before I could say
A word, I was on the ground as well,
Goin' like the hammers o' hell!
'Twas only then I saw where I was.
On my mother's grave! But that was no cause
For panic, though I was a bit
Upset at first by the strangeness of it.
The Knockanore woman was happy as Larry,
And I was sparkin' and merry
As a cricket. 'Yerra, you might
As well enjoy the gift o' the night
While you have the chance,' I said
To myself, realisin' the dead are dead,
Past holiness and harms—
And the livin' woman was in my arms.

'Twas great fun
While it lasted, and it lasted long. The sun
Was startin' to climb the sky when we rose
Up and settled our clothes.
'How are you, girl?' says I.
'Yerra, fine,' says she.
''Twas a fine night,' says I.
''Twas so, but a bit cold towards mornin',' says she
'And I wouldn't mind a hot cup o' tay
This minute.' 'You're a wise woman,' I said,
'Let them say whatever they say,
There's wan thing sure. 'Tis hard to bate the cup o' tay.'
And then, 'Whisht,' I said,
Suddenly remembering the quiet dead.
With the memory, I started to sing,
Then and there, a bar of a jig,
And as I sang I danced as well
On the body whose soul was in heaven or hell.
'You're a gay man,' says she, 'to bring
Me to a place like this for your bit of a fling,

The Dingle Peninsula, County Kerry, is studded with hermit dwellings, churches, standing stones and crosses. This Calvary group, on Slea Head, can be seen from many miles out to sea.

Above *Anti-amendment campaigners demonstrating in March 1983, when a small but influential group of right-wing Catholics persuaded both main parties (Fianna Fail and Fine Gael) to support a constitutional amendment preventing abortion from being made legal.*

And I'm thinkin' the love has gone to your head
When you dance a jig on the bones o' the dead.'
Said I, 'By the Christ that is divine,
If I have a son may he dance on mine.
While the man has the chance he should dance and
sing,' I said,
'For he'll be the hell of a long time dead.
So come on now without further ado
And I'll put on the kettle for the tay.'
She smiled and we started on our way
In the early light that was breakin' for day.
The night was lost, the daylight stretched ahead,
Behind me slept the unforgettable dead,
Beside me stepped a woman with gamey eye,
Laughin' as the sun mounted the sky.

Freedom, political, sexual, and other kinds, is dear to every Irish person's heart. In the relationship between the majority of Irish people and the Church this matter of freedom is always a touchy problem. No matter how the Church tries to fetter the freedom of its people, it will never really work because the love of freedom is as deep in the Irish as their insular identity itself. The two are, in fact, inseparable. Free and distinct; that is, after all, what any human being should be, or should try to be.

I sometimes think that the phrase "Thou shalt not" will never really work with the Irish because too many of them like to think in terms of "Thou shalt." I think of lines from my

favorite poet, William Blake. The poem is called *The Garden of Love.*

I went to the Garden of Love,
And I saw what I never had seen:
A Chapel was built in the midst
Where I used to play on the green.

And the gates of this Chapel were shut,
And "Thou Shalt Not" writ over the door:
So I turned to the Garden of Love
That so many sweet flowers bore.

And I saw it was filled with graves,
And tombstones where flowers should be:
And Priests in black gowns were walking their rounds
And binding with briars my joys and desires.

Despite the recurring horrors of history, despite our appalling social and economic problems, despite the tendency of decent men to fall for the temptation to exercise spiritual tyranny over other men and women, I still believe that Ireland possesses within itself the ability to grow into a true Garden of Love. (As I write these words, I can hear the cynics sneering.) Yes, there are signs that this growth may happen. The increasing independence of women is one of these signs. They are *questioning* men's facile pronouncements on everything relating to their lives. Many men are learning to respect, even love, this independence. Another sign is that Church and State are learning to respect the integrity of each other's separateness.

Whichever way you look at it, the days of the Great Male Conspiracy, in its various forms and deformities, are numbered. And a very good thing, for female and male alike.

What I am saying is that many of the Irish sicknesses concerning sex can be cleared up if we realize that religion has as much, or more, to learn from sex as sex has from religion. The gates of the Garden of Love are still open despite all our best efforts to bang them shut, and to keep them shut.

I know that in their heart of hearts the vast majority of Irish people want to enter that Garden.

And now is as good a time as any.

Below *Young Catholics gather on Ballybrit racecourse outside Galway City in 1979 for an open-air Mass conducted by Pope John Paul.*

Right *The Aran islanders do not claim to be 'true Celts,' although born and bred in the extreme west of Ireland. Their ancestry is very mixed.*

Faces of Ireland 6

Brendán O hEithir

It is important to keep in mind, when discussing the Irish character, that the island is very small: a mere 300 miles from its northernmost extremity to the far south, and little more than half that distance from east coast to west.

This "little room," in the words of W.B. Yeats, that led to "great hatred," contains a remarkable variety of landscape, with people who speak in a Babel of accents and some in two languages, the ancestral Irish as well as the more universal English.

Their ancestry is also reflected in their physical characteristics, their religious and social practices and in their customs. The diversity of their origins and the cultural forces to which they were subjected at various stages in history cause contradictions which, to some, are the yeast and salt in the national cake. Others, particularly those who like to reduce complex subjects to convenient generalizations, find these contradictions irritating and confusing.

Despite the work done by serious historians, film makers and the more perceptive travel writers, these convenient generalizations still abound to confuse rather than illuminate the path of the curious traveler. He who comes to observe the witty, golden-tongued Irish in full flight of fancy in a typical village pub, would do well to choose carefully.

Once, in the Antrim village of Portglenone, I sat for a good half-hour one night and observed five men contemplating the froth on their glasses of stout and the loudly ticking pub clock, during the course of which witticisms of this nature were exchanged:

"Brave an' coul' the night."

"Ach, aye."

"Brave an' coul' surely."

"Aye indeed, for the time o' year."

"Ach, aye, surely."

"No change, neither."

"Divil the change."

The drinkers were typical Irishmen of a certain regional culture and social class, as sparing of words as they were of the money in their pockets.

On the other hand, the traveler could just as easily happen upon a gaggle of men hunched against the gable of a public house in the west of Ireland, filling the air with nervous eloquence and mirth as they wait impatiently for pub opening time. These men would be typical of another social class and regional culture. To them, pleasant survival in a precarious world is far more important than any ethic concerning the work that may or may not be done on the morrow. It would also be true to say that a substantial majority of the population would fall between these two rather extreme

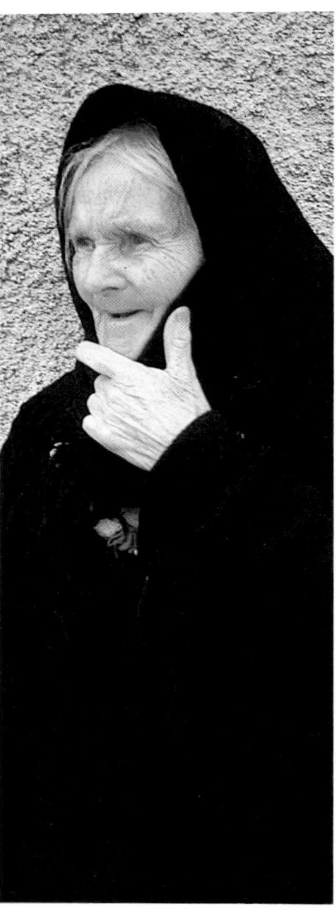

Above *Many Irish countrywomen still wear black.*

stools and lie there somewhat anonymously, dully, contentedly....

The pint pot that is the island of Ireland has been forced to contain within it a veritable gallon of plunderers, colonizers, missionaries of different kinds, adventurers, refugees of various persecuted denominations and seekers after the wisdom that is believed to exist on the extremities of continents. All of them left some mark; very few of their shadows have faded without trace.

People take me for a typical Celt. "Ah! An Aran Islander!" they cry. "How very interesting. At last a *real* Irishman." But how real is "real," even in the case of one whose neighboring parish to the west is on the shores of America? I fear that when Robert Flaherty made *Man of Aran* he sent a cluster of myths into orbit and not all of them have burnt up on re-entry.

Without overburdening the reader with details, let us take a short-cut through the history of Aran. The Celts, having retreated to the extremities of Western Europe, are credited by some archeologists with having built the large stone forts that dominate the island on which I grew up. Others give credit to the rather shadowy tribe that preceded them: archeology, like anthropology and psychiatry, can sometimes be an intriguingly inexact discipline.

After the Christianization of Ireland and the Danish and Norman invasions, Aran became, in turn, a great monastic settlement, a small prize in a power struggle between the warring Irish clans of O'Brien and O'Flaherty, an Elizabethan garrison, a Cromwellian prison, part of a landlord's fief and, from the end of the nineteenth century, a shrine for writers, linguists, archeologists, folklorists and would-be worshippers of the national and cultural taproot. Then, after three decades of independence, came the exact scientists. They sampled our blood, took impressions of our teeth, measured our heads and frames and went away to analyse their findings. To the consternation of those who had taken it upon themselves to categorize us as "true Celts," it was found that the typical islander closely resembled, in stature and in the structure of blood and bone, the native of East Anglia in England, and that his teeth closely resembled those of a typical Cockney from London.

The islanders, in fact, were displaying the signs of their hybrid heritage. The findings cheered them greatly for they removed that far more feared stigma of an inbred society.

Some anthropologists, who later came to study our social habits, were inclined to regard our blessings as mixed. One of them wrote in the American journal *Psychology Today* in February 1971 that although he found no evidence of "childlessness based on the sexual ignorance of spouses," nevertheless the people were blissfully ignorant of many uncommon sexual practices.

Which only goes to show that a fairly variegated people can survive for centuries on a remote rock in the Atlantic without any of the more spectacular characteristics of the personae in a Harold Robbins novel. What it tells us about the science of anthropology scarcely calls for comment.

But not all of the national genes were scrambled so successfully. Some tribes arrived, conquered modest spoils and then sat fast on their gains until the present day, learning nothing and forgetting even less. Not by his Twelfth of July regalia alone (bowler hat, dark suit, sash and walking stick) shall the Northern Ireland Orangeman be known, but by the constancy and purity of his genes also. For the Northern Ireland situation is an example of diversity leading not to richness, contradiction and change, but to polarization, suspicion and stagnation. When one takes away the bombs, the guns and the ferocious words, that basic dilemma remains.

Not all national minorities have been as introverted as the descendants of the seventeenth-century Northern planters. The Quakers and the Huguenots left their mark in Dublin and in the midland counties in a manner disproportionate to their numbers. The Jacobs,

Left *Rural life in Ireland is much the same as it has always been.*

Below *Putting to sea in a curragh. Once used all around the Irish coast, the curragh is now largely confined to the western seaboard.*

LOL

Bewleys, Goodbodys and Odlums are among the most respected in the world of business and industry. Many of them, without sacrificing their principles or individuality, became deeply involved in social affairs as well.

A character in Joyce's *Ulysses* remarks that the Irish never persecuted the Jews, they just never let them come in. They certainly did not come in great numbers, but they did form active communities in Dublin, Belfast and Cork. To a greater extent than any of the other national minorities, Jewish involvement in Irish politics during and after the struggle for independence was unequivocal and sustained.

As well as providing two of the most popular and outspoken mayors of Dublin and Cork, several members of the present Dáil (parliament) come from Dublin's small Jewish community. And, as if to prove their allegiance to different streams of political thought, they represent all the major political parties. While too much can be made of individual examples in any society, it would be fair as well as necessary to say that in public life in the Republic of Ireland it is what a person stands for, rather than his religion, ancestry or social standing, that matters when people are asked to vote for him.

That it is necessary to say this is in itself a comment on the face and mind of Ireland today. No other European state, not even newly united Germany, can match, for sheer self-consciousness, the current great debate on "Irishness" and the comparative importance of the various elements it contains. It is an acrimonious debate, at times a dialogue of the deliberately deaf, but it does serve to concentrate more open and reflective minds on what is divisive and what could be conducive to mutual understanding and peace in Irish life.

The ancestral language of this island is Irish (sometimes called Gaelic), a close cousin of Scots Gaelic and Manx, and a bit further removed from Welsh, Breton and Cornish. The Irish language began to die at the beginning of the seventeenth century, but what many generations thought to be its final death rattle proved to be a clearing of the throat for yet another final rally.

The modern revival of the Irish language was mainly due to the efforts of a small group of Protestant scholars who founded the Gaelic League almost a century ago. Chief among them was Dr. Douglas Hyde, who became first president of Ireland in 1938. He saw the language as a cultural unifying force in the

Far left *On 12 July each year the Orangemen of Northern Ireland, wearing the traditional sash of the Orange Order, celebrate King Billy's victory at the Battle of the Boyne.*

Below left *Sligo schoolboys dawdle on the way home. In the Great Famine of the 1840s, Sligo town lost a third of its population through death and emigration.*

Above *Traditional crafts are thriving. Here wool is spun on a home-made wheel prior to weaving.*

island, but, despite his efforts, his organization became part of the struggle for national independence. This, in turn, led many Northern Unionists to regard the ancestral language as another manifestation of the firm whose aim was to deprive the Unionists of their political power and take them over. The fact that the island's first daily newspaper in Irish is published in Belfast merely reinforces their suspicions.

In the Republic the Irish language is described in the Constitution as "the first official language" and is an obligatory subject in schools, although no longer a failing subject in public examinations. The reality of this rather large assumption is that a man was recently sent to prison for contempt of court because he demanded a trial through the medium of Irish in the Donegal Gaeltacht ("Gaeltacht" is the official term for the areas where Irish is the first language of the community and where the government conducts its affairs in Irish.)

Needless to say, the contradictions between the official attitude to the language and reality has given rise to much acrimony and occasional ribaldry. In the Republic an emerging middle class would like the language to crawl away and die. They regard it as an anachronism and an impediment to their chief ambition: the accumulation of wealth and equal partnership in the English-speaking world. But as the country is already English-speaking anyway, their case has a hollow ring and the Irish language seems likely to survive for a while longer—certainly for another two or three generations at least.

And whatever one may think of the efforts to revive it, the ancestral language is the most distinctively native (Celtic or Irish if you wish) manifestation of the continuity of life on the island. The fact that it is still a controversial matter, about which very patriotic citizens have mixed feelings, signifies a certain lust for life against the force of logic. It is also a very good reason for the traveler to avoid getting involved in arguments concerning its usefulness in the modern world.

Traditional Irish music should, on the face of it, be one of the great unifying forces in Ireland. To those who, rightly, regard it as one of the great folk music traditions of modern times, it may come as a surprise to learn that it almost died out in the third and fourth

Below *Swimmers from all over Dublin take part in the mile-long Liffey swim in August. The event is sponsored by the Electricity Supply Board.*

Left *Horse-trading is a serious business. Country horse fairs and races are held all over Ireland.*

Telefón
BAR
CLEARY
PROVISION

decades of this century. Neglect and a concerted effort to kill native entertainment in the homes of rural Ireland combined to drive the musicians, their music and the traditional set dances virtually underground.

The Catholic clergy, who could spot an occasion of sin before the thought entered the mind of the potential sinner, decided that dancing should take place under their eyes as far as was humanly possible. The traditional dances in houses, with music provided by local pipers, fiddlers and flute-players, were declared to be undesirable. For one thing they were not clerically supervised and, although the pastoral letters of the day cloak the unworthy thought in flowery language, it was clearly inferred that the perpendicular pleasures of the Irish kitchen dance might lead to horizontal dalliance which could prove detrimental to body and soul, not to mention the good name of the country.

Above *The sole survivor of Lord Hillsborough's Private Army, County Down, a garrison of 20 men and a sargent disbanded in 1890. The uniform is similar to that worn by the Dutch guards of William of Orange.*

Left *In country areas, the local pub often doubles as the local shop.*

So it came to pass that almost every parish in rural Ireland, as well as most of the smaller towns, sprouted gray concrete ghastlinesses known as parochial halls. The faithful were encouraged to attend these places of entertainment where jazzbands provided the music, where proper behavior was enforced by a properly trained cleric and where the takings swelled the parish funds.

It was very moral and it also was good business. Indeed so keen was the competition between two neighboring parochial halls that a strange story circulated through the length and breadth of Ireland (it has been calculated that it takes five days for a good rumor to travel, by word of mouth, from Malin Head in Donegal to

Right *The fiddler with his traditional music attracts quite a crowd, even in the face of more modern competition.*

Mizzen Head in Cork) during the early 1950s.

It concerned a young and innocent girl attending her first dance in one of the rival halls and the handsome young man who charmed her. She felt powerless in his arms and did not seem able to control her feelings as he tried to lure her to his car. Just as she was about to succumb she looked down, screamed loudly, crossed herself and fainted. The charming young man, whose cloven hoof had scared her out of more than a year's growth, vanished in a puff of sulfur through the roof of the dance hall. A year later the grass was growing in its car park and the birds were nesting in its rafters. The success of the state of business in the rival hall can be left to the imagination.

Above *A busker playing the uilleann or elbow pipes. The basic assembly consists of a bag, bellows, and chanter, but virtuoso players also use regulators and drones.*

Right *Sizing up the horses at a fair in Listowel, County Kerry. Listowel also hosts an annual writers' festival.*

Radio Eireann (as the national broadcasting service was then called) decided to record what was left of the traditional music and broadcast the best of it. In so far as the revival of a vanishing tradition can be attributed to a single action, Radio Eireann can claim credit for the astonishing hold that music, song and dance took on the young people of Ireland in the late 1950s and early 1960s. The fact that the revival coincided with a period of affluence and greater social freedom, as well as a slowing down in the rate of emigration to Britain and the United States, provided an additional impetus.

An organization called Comhaltas Ceoltóir Eireann (Federation of Irish Musicians) was

founded to foster the revival, and one of its first acts was to organize great gatherings of musicians called Fleadh Cheoil (literally a feast of music). These gatherings, at country and provincial level, drew great crowds and the annual All-Ireland Fleadh began to attract attendances of almost 100,000. Most of these yearly pilgrims were teenagers.

Social commentators as well as one poet, at least, date the birth of the new attitude to culture, tradition and morals from the All-Ireland Fleadh Cheoil of 1963 which was held over the Whit weekend in the midland town of Mullingar. The town was packed, there was music to be heard everywhere, indoors and out, but there was little or no disorder. On the

Right *Skilled repairs to the roof of a country cottage.*

Monday morning the local bishop condemned the event from the pulpit as a reprehensible and immoral gathering. After that, Comhaltas Cioltóir Eireann could only go from success to success; which it did, although the All-Ireland Fleadh suffered briefly from the modern world-wide phenomenon of mindless and destructive teenage thuggery.

It is impossible to write at any length about social life in Ireland without discussing drink. From birth to the final descent to the grave, drink is a constant factor at all Irish occasions. Contemporary historians have noted the Celtic fondness for great quantities of wine and how Celtic feasts often turned into bloody fights originating in boastful bragging concerning strength and valor.

Without wishing to be fanciful, let me bear witness to the fact that the Irish funeral is probably the most uniquely original and peaceful social occasion. Weddings frequently culminate in disorder, aided and abetted by the demon drink, but the funeral seems to bring out everything that is best in a complex nature. Not to give the departed a good, highly lubricated send-off is a grave social lapse on the part of family and friends, and one which will be remembered for years.

It is not surprising, therefore, that drink plays a large part in these congregations of musicians, aficionados and camp followers. Mullingar was my first All-Ireland Fleadh and I had the benefit of a local guide's knowledge as well as the hospitality of his home, no small

Left *On-course betting is an integral part of a day at the races. Large numbers of bookmakers attend most race meetings.*

matter in a town where every available bed was let out at the rate of a small apartment. During the weekend he drew my attention to a small middle-aged man, dressed in a mildewed suit, once respectable, a hard hat and a Guinness-stained shirt, once white. He moved from pub to pub, always alone, always drinking stout out of the bottle. He never got tipsy, let alone drunk, and the only change in his appearance in the course of the weekend was the steady growth of ginger fleece on his mottled face.

"A hard case," said my friend. "His wife and children have left and there can be very little left now from the proceeds of the second farm. Two shops, two farms and a gravel pit. That's serious drinking for you. But a decent little man and it's nice to see him enjoying himself."

On Tuesday morning, as Mullingar emptied and as the newspapers carried full reports of the bishop's denunciation, my friend and I met for a parting glass in a hotel in the center of the

Right *Good talk, on every subject under the sun, is part of Irish life.*

Below *Teenagers in Ireland today have greater expectations than their predecessors.*

HEEHAN
LISMIRE
Pilgrimage to Knock –
Sunday 20 July –
Player's

Right *Youngsters on a modern estate in Ballymun, Dublin.*

Above *Everyone dresses up for Nations Cup Day, the high point of the Dublin Horse Show.*

town. The traveling salesmen were moving west after the long weekend and, with the prurience which seems to be the hallmark of their calling in all countries, they sought details of the great feast of immorality they had missed by returning dutifully to the bosom of their families.

Already a rumor was circulating in Dublin about a young man who, on the sweltering Sunday afternoon, had taken his pleasure with his willing lady on the banks of the canal, jumped in for a swim and been instantly stricken in his prime and mortal sinfulness. Did it really happen? Tell us! Tell us more!

Standing quietly beside me, the little man with the ginger fuzz signified that a helping hand with the price of a bottle of stout would be appreciated. Having thanked me civilly and having satisfied his obvious need, he spoke at length for the first time.

"What's all this talk about it being a bad Fleadh? I came into town at midday on Friday and I've walked the length of it umpteen times since—scarce closed an eye for more than an hour or two—and do you know what I'm going to tell you now? I've seen no immorality at all. And I'll tell you something else. I think it was a great Fleadh. Only for the cursed music it would have been better than the Galway Races."

The faces of Ireland are not clearly seen. They are always slightly out of focus. This, as well as making them more interesting, is a reflection of what went before and what is happening now. For the only thing one can say with total certainty about the island of Ireland and its inhabitants is that it is—and will probably remain so for many years—unfinished business.

Right *Irish rugby goes from strength to strength. In the 1991 World Cup the Irish team lost to the Australians by a whisker in the quarter finals.*

Sporting Obsessions 7

Sean Kilfeather

When Barry McGuigan beat Eusebio Pedroza for the world featherweight boxing title in 1985, it was said that the Irish took over London, the scene of the fight, for the night. A London publican, still serving drinks to swaying, singing Irishmen at midnight, well past official closing time, was asked was he not afraid of a visit from the police. "On a night like this, they wouldn't dare come into the place," he said.

Such scenes were repeated in every part of Ireland, but the excitement of that evening was totally eclipsed when the streets of Dublin and Belfast were jammed with cheering crowds as McGuigan toured them in an open-topped bus, bringing business to a halt. In Dublin the crowds were so vast that the local police said they had experienced nothing like it since the Pope's visit in 1979.

Those Dublin scenes were in 1987 repeated when cyclist Stephen Roche, himself a Dubliner, won the Tour de France, the pinnacle of world cycling achievement. Again the bus, the milling crowds, bands and bunting, public receptions and widespread national rejoicing.

After the extraordinary jubilation that greeted the return of McGuigan and Roche, Dubliners thought they would never see the likes again—the apogee of sporting high spirits had been reached. They were wrong. In 1988, for the European Championships, and again in 1990, for the World Cup, it took the Irish soccer team close on three hours to get from Dublin airport to the center of the city, a journey of a mere eight miles, as the crowds swarmed around their bus, reducing its speed to a crawl. A crowd of 250,000, half the population of Dublin if the estimate is correct, turned out when the team came back from Italy. And the oddest thing about such adulation was that neither team won either tournament. In the World Cup the Irish team did not even win a match, only sneaking past Romania on a penalty "shoot-out."

But the teams caught the imagination of the Irish sporting public and gave a good account of themselves against Italy, England and Holland, the élite teams of world soccer. That was enough to bring Irish fans onto the streets. For hours after each game was over, city center traffic was in turmoil, lights flashed; horns blared and supporters danced and sang on the tops of moving cars. The carnival had come to town.

Thousands of supporters followed the team to Italy and traveled up and down the country, finally fetching up in Rome for the quarter final match with Italy. The match was narrowly lost but the fans stayed on in the Olympic Stadium,

Above *A muddy but unbowed Philip Matthews, captain of the Irish rugby team.*

singing and chanting the names of their heroes until the players came back onto the pitch to acknowledge their adoration.

Back home, there was blanket coverage of every match on television and the newspapers produced special editions and supplements with color pictures to satisfy a public insatiable for every bit of information they could get. Prime Minister Charles Haughey and several members of his Cabinet traveled to Rome. Any politician who ignored the football risked his seat in the Dáil.

Soccer has a bad reputation in Europe as far as crowd behavior is concerned. British clubs were banned from European competition for several years after a British crowd rioted in Belgium, causing dozens of deaths among Italian supporters. German, Dutch and Italian football fans have also earned notoriety.

Not so the Irish. Frequently confused in the Continental mind with the British (all of the Irish players play for British clubs), the Irish were expected to be loutish, violent and vulgar and, at first, both in Germany in 1988 and in Italy in 1990, were treated with a suspicion bordering on fear. Soon, however, their jolly, witty and joyful behavior charmed the locals. While the English were refused service in bars and restaurants and treated with contempt by police and municipal officials, the Irish were made welcome everywhere.

They sang and they danced and frequently got drunk but every group policed itself and anyone who stepped out of line was disciplined by his peers. They spent large sums of money, tipped bar and restaurant staff outrageously, and supported the team with total dedication. They left behind them a captivated audience, so much so that the Irish Tourist Board reported an immediate increase in the number of holiday inquiries from Italy. This was reflected in a significant influx of Continental visitors in the summer of 1991.

It is widely accepted in Ireland that the public has very catholic tastes in sport. Those who went to Italy for the soccer World Cup came from a very wide spectrum of society and included businessmen, bankers, lawyers, teachers, farmers, plumbers, carpenters, laborers and indeed many unemployed. There was also a very high proportion of women supporters.

A similar cross-section is to be seen at hurling matches and at rugby internationals in Dublin, Edinburgh or Paris. Many Irish sports fans are members of golf clubs. Players who are prominent in rugby football are seen in big numbers at race meetings or at Gaelic football matches or watching schoolboy soccer.

The Gaelic Athletic Association (GAA) controls the games of hurling and Gaelic football. It was established in 1884 by people of a patriotic caste of mind who felt that the sports of the English were dominating Irish athletic life and that the traditional Irish pastimes and games were suffering as a result.

In the years that followed, Irish politics went through many phases. The link with Britain was always a matter of contention in the social and sporting life of the country and the GAA was frequently accused of being a quasi-political force, an allegation that still persists to some extent. However, the games of Gaelic football and hurling were preserved by the GAA and are now the two games most widely played and supported in the country. The Association has remained fiercely amateur; although it is by far the richest sporting organization in the country.

In the summer of 1991 a preliminary match between Meath and Dublin, in a competition to find the All-Ireland Gaelic football champions, ended in a draw on three occasions and a fourth match was needed in order to reach a verdict. The total official attendance for the four matches was 237,377 paying customers, representing a take of some £1,055,000. All of that money, after expenses, was plowed back into providing facilities, equipment and coaching for the native games. Because of the unique element of the tie, one sole concession was made: the players were treated to a sunshine holiday in the winter but no match fees of any kind were paid.

Sports are so closely woven into the fabric of Irish life that even those who are not really interested in sporting endeavor are unprepared to admit their ignorance publicly. One of the criticisms levelled at former prime minister Garret FitzGerald was that he once admitted

Right *Irish cycling hero Stephen Roche during a stage of the Tour de France in 1987. As if winning the Tour was not enough, he also won the Giro d'Italia and the World Championships that year.*

VAGABOND
TOSHIBA
CREDIT
LOOK
PEUGEOT
11

that he would prefer to study a train timetable or a balance sheet rather than watch a football game. Was it this unguarded statement that cost him several points in a subsequent popularity poll? His credibility slumped further when he admitted that he didn't know what colors were worn by the Cork hurling team.

Sporting heroes are legion in folklore, in history and in song. A certain Thady Quill is immortalized in a ballad:

In the great hurling match between Cork and
Tipperary,
'Twas played in a field on the banks of the Lee.
Our own darlin' hurlers afraid of being beaten.
They sent for bould Thady to Ballinagree.

Yerra he hurled the ball right and left in their faces
And showed the Tipperary lads training and skill.
If they trod near his lines shure he swore he would
maim them.
And the papers were full of the praise of Thad Quill.

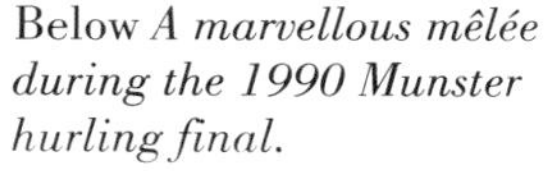

Below *A marvellous mêlée during the 1990 Munster hurling final.*

For ramblin' for rovin' for football or courtin'
For drinking black porter as fast as you fill.
In all your day's rovin' you'll find none so jovial
As the Muskerry sportsman the bould Thady Quill.

The sporting ballad has become something of an institution in Ireland and, as with all Irish institutions, there is a mischievous tale to be told about it. The real-life Thady (Irish for the Biblical Thadeus) Quill was, it appears, far from being a person of talent in any field, least of all sport.

Laughter and mischief are never far away from the sporting scene. Although sports are deadly solemn at times, a smile is always lurking on the other side of the face. As Tony O'Reilly, a brilliant international rugby football player and later president of the Heinz corporation, once said: "The condition of Irish sport is frequently desperate but never serious."

There is plenty of evidence in mythology and not a little in history to indicate that organized games took place in Ireland long before the ancient Olympic Games. The Tailteann Games, a program of sporting events in honor of Queen Tailte of the "Kingdom of Meath" just north of Dublin, were organized in 632 BC. Running, jumping, throwing the spear or javelin and hurling were all on the bill. The old Irish legends relate that admission to the Fianna, Fionn MacCumhail's traveling militia, was allowed only to those who excelled in such sporting pursuits. And the historian Brother Liam P. O Caithnia has, in his research, come across references to hurling and other games in the ancient Brehon Laws, in the sagas of the Red Branch Knights and in the *Fenian* or *Ossianic Cycle* of legends.

It is a somewhat refined version of hurling that survives and thrives in Ireland today, attracting as many as 70,000 spectators to the top contests. A distinctively Irish game, it is contested with great fervor and élan. Sometimes wild, sometimes as smooth and elusive as gossamer, many commentators have been moved to describe it as an art form. Played with a leather-covered ball about the same size as a tennis ball and with curved sticks fashioned with great skill and care from the roots of ash trees, its speed is bewildering

Left *Hand-to-hand combat during the All-Ireland hurling final in 1989. The match is held in Dublin on the first Sunday in September.*

Above *The legendary Alex 'Hurricane' Higgins, moody genius of the snooker table and winner of countless international competitions.*

Right *If anything, Gaelic football is even more popular than hurling. The All-Ireland championships take place through the summer, with the final being played on the third Sunday in September.*

to the uninitiated. The ball flies from one end of the field to the other, driven through the air or on the ground with dexterity and blinding speed.

It was at this game that another former prime minister, Jack Lynch, excelled, winning five All-Ireland medals with Cork in the 1940s and 1950s. But even he pales as a hero before the challenge of his team-mate Christy Ring, around whom legends have grown up and about whom books have been written and to whom a life-sized statue has been erected. Not even a prime minister can be as famous as Christy Ring. His reputation for turning looming defeat into last-minute victory is also the stuff of balladry:

Now Cork are beat,
The hay is saved,
The Tippmen stoutly sing.*
You spoke too soon,
*My sweet gossoon,***
For here comes Christy Ring!

*Tipperary men **young man

Another hurling hero of earlier times was Tommy Daly, a doctor from County Clare. He was a goalkeeper. If you have to be a little mad to be a good hurler, you have to be completely insane to play in goal. In Daly's day goalkeepers were only slightly protected by the rules. Once the match started, "open season" was declared on goalkeepers. The only protection they had was a wall of bodies provided by their defending colleagues. Even now a goalkeeper has to have the eyes of a hawk, hands like a magnet, nerves of steel and bones of tungsten. The ball comes whizzing in at speeds of up to 70 or 80 miles an hour. It has to be stopped with stick or hand to prevent a goal and then driven away as opponents bear down, intent on creating mayhem. Goalkeepers are not concerned by that so much. Footwork and speed of thought can get a man out of trouble. What they really fear is the high ball dropping slowly into the goalmouth. Then the nerves and the eye are tested to the full. The ball will be the only focus of attention. Not until it is grab-

Below *General action during a women's football match between the Republic and Northern Ireland.*

bed out of the forest of ashen clubs can personal safety or concern for life and limb be taken into account.

Gaelic football, often described as a mixture of soccer, rugby and American gridiron, although it would probably be more correct to say that it is the begetter of them all, is a somewhat staid cousin of hurling but more widespread and popular. The big games in August and September at the conclusion of the All-Ireland championship in hurling and football take on the trappings of national occasions.

Rugby started out in Ireland as an exclusive Protestant and "garrison" game. Was the boy at Rugby College in England who is widely credited with having invented the game of rugby football by "taking up the ball and running with it" copying something he saw on holiday in Tipperary? His name, William Webb Ellis, appears on the trophy that goes to the winners of the rugby World Cup. The adoption of the game by Catholic upper-class schools changed the emphasis greatly and it is now a game for people of all backgrounds, politics and religions.

On the day of a rugby international in Dublin, Ireland shows a face to the world that indicates what a united Ireland might be like. Both on and off the field Catholic, Protestant, dissenter, Unionist and Republican, socialist and conservative, liberal and bigot mix into an attractive amalgam of faces, attitudes and accents. On the field Irish Army men and Royal Ulster Constabulary members play in the green, shamrock-sprigged shirts and stand shoulder to shoulder facing the Republic's Tricolor. Wolfe Tone, the eighteenth-century

Right *Sonia O'Sullivan, one of Ireland's top women athletes, runs to victory in the 1500 meters in the 1991 World Student Games.*

Below *Mary Peters, Ireland's most phenomenal woman athlete, won the women's pentathlon gold medal at the 1972 Olympics. An international-standard athletics track in Belfast is named after her.*

Protestant Irish patriot, would surely approve.

Sadly, attempts to repeat this in other sports have failed. Two international soccer teams are fielded in competitions like the World Cup. At club level in Northern Ireland sectarianism is rife at football games; two teams from Nationalist areas were forced out of soccer entirely. Songs of a sectarian nature are used to taunt opposition supporters: "We'll kick ten thousand Papishes all over Dolly's Brae" is one of the less offensive ditties.

A sectarian riot during a match between the Protestant Linfield team and Catholic Belfast Celtic in the late 1940s led to the withdrawal of the Celtic team from the game of soccer. The more recent strife in Northern Ireland also forced Derry City out of the game with the result that they have now joined the Republic's soccer league, which

means that they play in a competition which is outside the jurisdiction of the state in which they play their home games, a strangely Irish solution to an Irish problem.

The traditional games have given the Irish sports scene a unique flavor and a sturdy base on which to display the national character. But internationally, too, the Irish can be observed at play, notably on the athletics track, in the boxing ring and more recently in cycling where, for a small country, a very high standard has been set. In recent times, Eamon Coghlan dominated the indoor athletics scene in the United States and added the world outdoor 5000 meters championship to his list of victories at Helsinki in 1983. John Treacy won a silver medal in the marathon at the Los Angeles Olympics.

It was also in Los Angeles that Ireland notched up its finest Olympic achievement: in 1932 two Tipperary athletes won gold medals within an hour of each other—Pat O'Callaghan

in the hammer event and Bob Tisdall in the 400-meter hurdles. It was O'Callaghan's second gold medal, his first having been won in Amsterdam four years earlier. And in Melbourne in 1956 a lanky, goose-stepping young man from Wicklow called Ronnie Delaney beat the cream of the world's middle-distance runners to take the gold in the 1500 meters.

Throwing the hammer, said to be an Irish sport originally, was dominated by Irish athletes up until 1932, but many of them emigrated to the United States, so their medals were credited to their adopted country. O'Callaghan's second gold medal in the hammer event was Ireland's last such victory in the Olympic Games. Although O'Callaghan was a virtual certainty to win a third gold in the Berlin Olympics of 1936, politics intervened; because of a conflict between an athletics body which claimed jurisdiction over all of Ireland and another body which accepted

Below *Supporters from Cork succumb to the sunshine and euphoria of a hurling game.*

that Northern Ireland came under British control, there was no Irish participation of any kind. British "connivance" at this split has been resented ever since.

Frequent efforts have been made to heal this split, without any obvious success. Irish boxers from North and South compete in the Olympics under the Irish flag, while hockey players from Northern Ireland compete with Britain under the Union Jack. Another Irish solution to an Irish problem.

The native games of hurling and Gaelic football are not divided, mainly because they are of domestic importance only and because they are mainly confined, particularly in the North, to those of the Catholic-Nationalist tradition. The team representing the county of Down, which is in the North, has won the All-Ireland Gaelic football title on four occasions, the last being in 1991.

Below *The bones of Arkle, the 1960s champion steeplechaser, are exhibited in the National Stud museum at Kildare.*

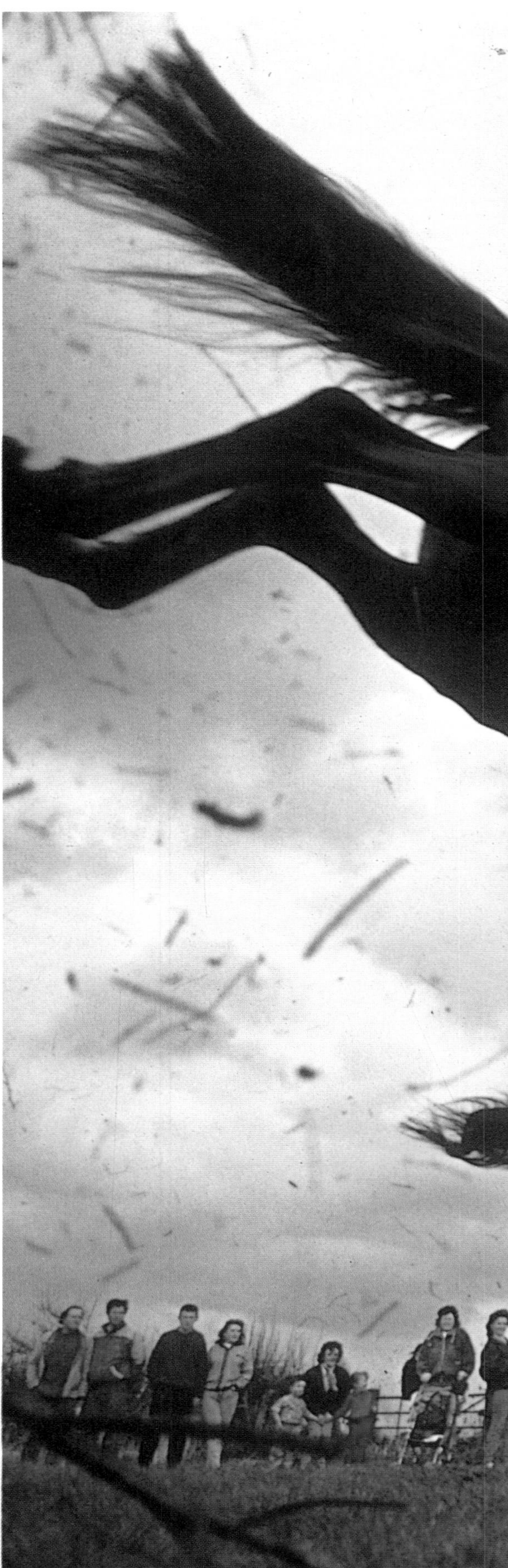

Right *Flying horses and flying turf during the Irish Grand National at Fairyhouse, County Meath.*

It is perhaps in the presence of horses and greyhounds that the Irish people reveal their innate sentimentality. Love for these animals is perhaps too mean a word; devotion might fit better. The bones of Arkle, one of the great steeplechasers, have been dug up and reassembled in skeleton form at the National Stud in Kildare. A statue to a great coursing greyhound, Master McGrath, stands by the roadside in Waterford.

10
5

Above *Jack Doyle, photographed here in 1936, was one of the great characters of Irish boxing in the 1930s.*

The top race meetings, at places like the Curragh, Leopardstown, Fairyhouse, Tralee and dozens of other tracks dotted around the country, are thronged even on working days. Thousands of people flock to Galway for a five-day meeting in July every year. Millions of pounds are wagered on the horses; poker games, with drinking and musicianship thrown in, go on all night. Cheltenham's Festival race meeting in England is also something of a pilgrimage for Irish racing enthusiasts.

Again, the mix of class and creed at race meetings is fully representative of all sections of a diverse community. Priests and paupers mingle with millionaires and charlatans; the presence of pickpockets is regarded as an inevitable, if undesirable evil. A day at the races is not just racing; it is living. Fortunes may be lost but there is always tomorrow, when one's luck will surely change.

The Irish have invented many words to convey ideas or impressions that the staid English language cannot handle. One such word is "crack," which may or may not have a Gaelic root. It means a variety of things, including laughter, song, drink, music, fun, rumor, gossip, sport and roguery. One Irishman who enjoyed "crack" to the ultimate was Jack Doyle, a swashbuckling Corkman who made a fortune with his fists in the boxing ring, spent it all on "crack," became a cabaret artist in sleazy London nightclubs and pubs and died penniless. He was a bit of a braggart, but a likeable rogue with a big heart in a big, handsome body. Once, during the height of his career as boxer-cum-entertainer, he boasted that he could sing like John McCormack and box like Jack Dempsey. When the boast was relayed to Dempsey, who had been heavyweight champion of the world, the scathing reply was: "I think the guy has gotten it the wrong way around."

Doyle was larger than life. He married the tempestuous movie star Movita and the streets of Dublin and Cork were jam-packed when he brought her home to show her off to the

Left *Show-jumping on Nations Cup Day at the Dublin Horse Show.*

Below *Enthusiastic spectators at Galway Races, held in the last week of July each year and the most important event in the Galway social calendar.*

neighbors. But high living, late nights and boxing don't mix. Doyle's horizontal approach to life both inside and outside the ring, drunk or sober, soon took their toll. Hundreds of men of his generation will tell you still of the half-crown Jack Doyle borrowed when he was down and out and parched for want of a drink.

Not all Irish boxers ended up like Doyle. The descendants of Irish parents, like Dempsey himself, John L. Sullivan and Gene Tunney made fortunes at the sport and are listed in the pantheon of great heavyweights. In a small pub in the town of Kilcullen in the county of Kildare the mummified arm of an old-style bare-knuckle boxer called Dan Donnelly is preserved in a glass case. It is stared at reverently by thousands of tourists while his exploits are recited for their benefit.

Not far away is the secluded small valley where one of the most famous events in the history of Irish sport took place. It was here in 1815, when boxing was a banned pursuit, that Dan Donnelly took on the pride of England, George Cooper, and beat him into subjection in

Left *Irish rowers are making their mark in international competition. Niall O'Toole, one of Ireland's hopes for the 1992 Olympics, won a gold medal in the lightweight single skulls at the World Championships in Austria in 1991.*

Below *The golf course at Ballybunion, County Kerry, lies beside sand and sea at the mouth of the River Shannon.*

PING

11 bloody rounds. More than 30,000 spectators crammed into the valley, which has been known ever since as "Donnelly's Hollow." But Donnelly, like Doyle, loved the bright lights and the fame that his exploits brought him. He was vulnerable to flattery and to the depredations of borrowers and boyos, and he succumbed to all this and to ill health as well before he could truly test his mettle against the top boxers of his day.

There are very few Irish people who have not at one time tried sport of one kind or another. Golf, like rugby, has become a game for the masses. Thousands of golfers flock to clubs at weekends and at first light take on the scores of top-class courses all over the country. Everyone wants to be as good as highly successful players like Christy O'Connor or Joe Carr and if they can't quite play as well as those two they will be sure to "talk a good game." Golf has also united Irishmen from North and South; players from both sides of the Border have represented Ireland together on the international scene with some success.

There is an urge in every Irishman to be a top sportsman; academic, financial or political success will always be regarded as secondary. A man who hasn't played hasn't quite made it in life.

This approach is epitomized in a tale about one Tom "Click" Brennan, who as a young man played fervent football for his native county of Sligo, frequently refered to as "the Yeats county." Some years ago, when "Click" was no longer young, he met a young hitchhiker with a pack on his back who wanted to know the road to Sligo town.

"Why do you want to go there?" Click asked.

"I'm going to the Yeats Summer School," the lad replied. "You know about Yeats? Sligo's most famous son. The Nobel prizewinner."

"Yeats? Yeats?" said Click, scratching his head, pretending not to know. "Famous Sligoman, was he? Well, I'll tell you this. Whoever he was, he never kicked a ball for Sligo."

Nobel Prizes for poetry are all very well but only sporting achievement can really answer an Irishman's true calling.

Left *Des Smyth, one of Ireland's most successful golfers over the last ten years, extricates himself from a bunker during the 1990 Irish Pro Golf Championship at Woodbrook, County Wicklow.*

Right *A collection of exquisitely tied trout flies. Most Irish rivers of any pretensions contain trout.*

Right *O'Connell Street, Dublin, in the small hours of the morning.*

To the Future 8

Brendan Kennelly

When Sir Nicholas Fenn, the imaginative, sensitive and hard-working former British Ambassador to Ireland, was asked what he thought were the reasons for Ireland's many problems, he replied that the old ancestral antagonisms were, in an absurd but tragic way, holding Ireland back. Asked whether he believed if peace will finally come to this troubled island, he answered that it definitely will, but that it will have to be worked for with dedication and patience.

Many Irish people would agree with that assessment.

Ancestral antagonisms.... Yes. And these antagonisms have for ages been deliberately perpetrated by a barbaric closed mind, as obvious in the bullish rhetoric of Ian Paisley in the North as in the stony words of various kinds of terrorists both north and south. Another way to express the slogan "No Surrender" is "Keep hatred alive!"

Yet there are signs that the mechanical, murderous activities prompted by the closed mind are at last being questioned and passionately protested against by ordinary but horrified people on both sides of the Border. The revolution against hatred is coming from that most unlikely person, the man in the street, Joe Soap. There have been several expressions of this kind of outraged feeling against the IRA. When a car driven by Daniel Lennon, an IRA man fatally wounded in an exchange of gunfire with the British Army, killed Andrew, Joanne and John Maguire, three children, as Lennon crashed into them on Finaghy Road North in Belfast, this led to the famous demonstrations by the Peace Women, and ultimately to the foundation of the Peace People Movement.

The Peace Women drew tens of thousands of supporters from different religious groups right across society and were often attacked by IRA supporters in Belfast.

But the biggest and most spectacular protest against IRA violence for nearly fifteen years occurred in early August 1991 when thousands of people in Cooley, County Louth, protested against the murder of a local farmer, Mr. Thomas Oliver, by the IRA for allegedly giving information concerning the IRA to the Irish police. Cardinal Daly called on the people to reject the IRA and its violence. His appeal met with a very positive response. It is clear by now that the vast majority of the people of Ireland want no part in and give no approval to the IRA's murderous tactics. The Cooley protest was a truly significant one in that it came from the ordinary country people of Ireland, perhaps the most conservative section of the Irish community. When the Irish country people make this kind of protest you can be sure that it is profoundly and passionately meant, because it has grown slowly, almost reluctantly, and with inexorable conviction. The protest at Cooley was absolutely *wrenched* from these people who, like the bulk of the Irish rural population, have always supported republicanism. But the IRA have, in the people's eyes, gone far beyond and away from the essential republican spirit, which has nothing at all to do with the mindless mayhem perpetuated by the IRA today. Ordinary people are saying to the IRA: "Look, we don't want you because you do not represent our feelings, our convictions, our aspirations. Stop it!" The IRA claim to represent these very people. Will they listen to them now?

No, is the short answer to that one.

Why? Because for many generations now, the roots of Ireland's continuing tragedy have been in Ireland's own closed mind.

What is this closed mind? It is rooted in history. The greater part of Ireland is a post-colonial land, but the effects of colonialism are still deeply buried and operative in the Irish psyche. In the South there is still a mechanical undercurrent of dislike for the English, while in the North there is a predominant, unquestioning sense of loyalty to the Crown. But it is not love of England that wins the loyalty of Ulster Unionists; it is fear and distrust of the Irish government and people. The attitudes of many people on both sides of the Border are characteristic of the closed mind, which is marked by a fierce and automatic resistance to alternatives and by an equally fierce assertion of its own limited but ferociously held viewpoints or beliefs. The closed mind oversimplifies reality in such a way that self-doubt is as unthinkable as a deep tolerance of the rights of others.

The closed mind leads to fanaticism.

A fanatic is a terrorist who is himself terrified of alternatives. A fanatic is a person who can see only one point of view and who

Below *The streets of Clifden, County Galway, come to life during the Connemara Pony Show. The town is perched high above the deep-sided estuary of the Owenglin River, with the magnificent Connemara Mountains as a backdrop.*

Left *The River Cullenagh tumbles over its bed of stony slabs in the market town of Ennistymon, County Clare.*

sincerely believes that most other points of view are not merely wrong but have to be exterminated. A fanatic will always try to bend reality to his own design. He will work with unrelenting energy and dedication to achieve this. He is strong and sincere. He may well be incapable of insincerity. And he has an even more powerful weapon to aid him in his "noble task," his "glorious enterprise," his "ancient conflict," his "great and unrelenting struggle." He has a mind that is completely closed, a truly terrifying weapon.

Until very recently, both the Roman Catholic Church and the Church of Ireland, the chief Protestant church, advocated and sustained the closed mind. But this is slowly changing thanks, among other things, to the increasing independence of women, the sense of cultural difference and complexity introduced by a well-educated and independent-minded new generation of young men and women. There is, above all, a sense that a Church, *any* Church, is not simply or solely composed of bishops and priests and nuns and various kinds of clerics; it is composed, above all, of people, its ordinary members. The ordinary people of Ireland are speaking out against the IRA. The ordinary people of Ireland are also determined to show their Churches that they are no longer a subservient peasantry but an independent, hard-working and civilized people capable of making their own decisions about public and private matters. The ordinary people of Ireland can be quite extraordinary at times.

The way forward in Ireland is marked by a strong sense of this new, growing ability of ordinary Irish people to make difficult decisions by themselves, without referring constantly to clerics who already have enough work to do, and who have plenty decisions of their own to make.

But evidence of this closed mind is still with us. The closed mind, though firm and resolute in itself, is in fact terrified of expression, especially of expression coming from "strangers," "oddballs" and "foreigners." Many of the "oddballs" have been Irish writers who tried to understand and express their country and its people. In the 1930s, 1940s and 1950s nearly every Irish writer worth his or

Left *In the slanting light of late afternoon, the Ireland of myth and romance comes very close.*

her salt was banned by the Censorship Board. Thanks be to God, the same Censorship Board seems to have censored itself into a state of non-existence, or at least of acceptable paralysis, at the moment. These men and women, intelligent and terrified, were the intellectual representatives of the closed mind. They produced almost nothing and banned a lot of good literature. They were apostles of mediocrity. An American friend of mine, an academic, once said to me: "If I wanted a good reading list of twentieth-century Irish writers, I think I'd simply give my students a list of all the books that have been banned in Ireland."

The closed mind never likes to rock the boat of its own security. In any sphere it hates and fears the thought or image of a possible rival. It wants power and dominance. It craves the conviction that it is the sole embodiment of the truth.

The mark of any soul is its capacity for growth. God never created anything that had not the potential for growth. It is sinful and criminal to restrict that potential, but that restriction is the function of the closed mind. In Northern Ireland, people are murdering each other with skill and dedication because they have closed minds. Catholic and Nationalist, Protestant and Unionist. Labels. Ireland is an island of labels. In that situation, a man is not a man but a label, and he will kill on behalf of his particular label.

It is necessary to grasp the intensity and strength of the closed mind. It does not question itself, but puts itself beyond the painful reach of self-doubt. It assumes that its own self is the center of rightness, of infallibility. It knows right and wrong, it judges, it concludes. And so it can kill with impunity and defend with integrity.

When Shakespeare wrote *Macbeth* he believed a murderer must have pangs of conscience. But then Shakespeare never came to Ireland, or perhaps never met the closed mind. If he did, he turned his back on it, and he was right. In Ireland you cannot turn your back on the closed mind because there is evidence of it everywhere.

Sport is one of the few areas where various forms of prejudice tend not to show themselves. When men and women confront each other in

Below *Author and playwright Brendan Behan (1923-1964) grew up in Dublin. His best-known works are the autobiographical novel* Borstal Boy, *and the plays* The Quare Fellow *and* The Hostage.

Right *The Financial Services Centre in Dublin stands beside the Custom House, a monument to an earlier age of trade and commerce. The most successful Irish companies today are multinationals. Ireland is also the base of Europe's biggest beef producer and the world's largest aircraft leasing company.*

sport they leave behind many of the prejudices that degrade and narrow their ordinary lives. Because sport is a matter of passion and skill, prejudice gets burned up in it like old newspapers at a children's bonfire. Sport purifies and ennobles. But in Ireland, sad to say, it has also shown the closed mind at work.

I will not dwell on this because the entire scene is changing. The Irish are a truly sports-loving people and are prepared to support practically any form of sport with concentration, enthusiasm and humor. And yet the GAA, the most powerful sporting body in Ireland, is still not opening itself as it should to the *entire* youth of Ireland. The old entrenchment in self still exists. One still hears the same weary platitudes and clichés trotted out at official meetings and social gatherings. Prejudice dies hard; and the closed mind often battles fiercely to stay closed.

In the 1940s and 1950s you could not—if you were a member of the GAA—attend rugby or soccer games. They were "English." They were "foreign." That seems incredible now. But that's precisely what I'm talking about. The old hatred of difference, of alternatives. Cut out everybody else, show your own strength, emphasize your own ignorance, underline your contempt, turn your sneer into a code of honor, close your mind.

Today's youngsters don't want that closed mind. On the whole, they reject it. On the whole.

James Joyce's short story, *The Dead*, brilliantly filmed some years ago by John Houston, concerns people with closed minds. Some critics have said this is the greatest short story in the English language, and there is an argument to be put forward in support of that evaluation. One thing, however, which cannot be denied, is that it succeeds brilliantly as a scrutiny of people who have shut their minds to everything except their own petty realities. The "hero" of the story, Gabriel Conroy, discovers this truth near the end when he catches a glimpse of himself in the mirror of the hotel bedroom where he has gone, after a party, with the intention of making love to his wife Gretta. But she, remembering a lover of many years ago, ignores him. Gabriel gets a glimpse of his

Below *Another of Dublin's famous sons, James Joyce (1882-1941), author of* Ulysses, Portrait of the Artist *and* Finnegans Wake, *spent most of his life on the Continent. This portrait of him was painted by Jacques-Emile Blanche. (National Portrait Gallery, London)*

closed, restricted life, a pathetic man who has been cut out of his wife's sexual being by the memory of a dead boy.

Since Joyce, many Irish writers have been savage and incisive in their attacks on this narrowness, this castrating, claustrophobic puritanism. People like John McGahern, Edna O'Brien, Hugh Leonard, John Broderick, Brendan Behan and John B. Keane as well as younger writers like Dermot Bolger, Mary Leland, Kate Cruise O'Brien, Maeve Kelly, Paula Meehan, Roddy Doyle, Michael Curtin and others, many of them young, angry, articulate women, have lashed out at the constricting and debilitating effects of the closed minds and hearts of Ireland.

Left *Stormont Castle, completed in 1932 and located on the east side of Belfast, was the seat of the Northern Irish government until 1972, when direct rule was imposed from Westminster.*

Above *Following tradition, Irish President Mary Robinson presents the Agha Khan trophy at the 1991 Dublin Horse Show.*

It is a singular irony that women, who were for so long the victims of the closed mind, especially in marriage, but also all through society, have now become some of the most powerful critics of its effects and consequences.

The face that Ireland is at last opening up is due in considerable measure to these strong-minded women. It is also due to a few personalities on radio and television, notably Gay Byrne whose programs have opened up for public discussion topics that hitherto seemed not merely unspeakable but unthinkable. This man has done some great work.

I think it is fair to say that Irish writers have nearly always stood up for freedom of expression. Sean O'Faolain and Peadar O'Donnell,

Above *The starkly beautiful Burren in County Clare allows subsistence farming only.*

Right *A tanker nears completion in Belfast's Harland & Wolff shipyard.*

who edited *The Bell*, a fiery, inquiring, open-minded publication, are a good example of this. So are Frank O'Connor, the towering Yeats and Joyce, and poets such as Louis MacNeice, Patrick Kavanagh and Austin Clarke. Austin Clarke, especially, had the searing eye of the satirist for the terrified respectability of the closed mind. The following poem concerns the burial of an Irish president, Dr. Douglas Hyde, a Protestant, a fine scholar, folklorist and translator of Irish poetry. In this poem, Hyde's body lies in St. Patrick's Cathedral, a beautiful Protestant cathedral in Dublin where the great Dean Swift who "served human liberty" once ministered and is buried. Outside the cathedral lurk members of the Irish government, hiding, because Catholics committed grave sin if they ventured into Protestant centers of worship. This poem, *Burial Of An Irish President*, is one of the most savage indictments of that closed mind which has so effectively impeded the progress and development of Ireland.

The tolling from St Patrick's
Cathedral was brangled, repeating
Itself in top-back room
And alley of the Coombe,
Crowding the dirty streets,
Upbraiding all our pat tricks.
Tricoloured and beflowered,
Coffin of our President,
Where fifty mourners bowed,
Was trestled in the gloom
Of arch and monument,
Beyond the desperate tomb
Of Swift. Imperial flags,
Corunna, Quatre Bras,
Inkermann, Pretoria,
Their pride turning to rags,
Drooped, smoke-thin as the booming
Of cannon. The simple word
From heaven was vaulted, stirred
By candles. At the last bench
Two Catholics, the French
Ambassador and I, knelt down.
The vergers waited. Outside,
The hush of Dublin town,
Professors of cap and gown,
Costello, his Cabinet,
In Government cars, hiding
Around the corner, ready
Tall hat in hand, dreading
Our Father *in English. Better*
Not hear that "which" for "who"
And risk eternal doom.

To illustrate the ways in which Ireland is changing for the better, it is interesting to compare the furtive taoiseach (prime minister) of that poem, Mr. Costello, with today's enlightened taoiseach, Mr. C. J. Haughey, whose interest in the arts, and in the rights of artists to be critics of society, led him to help found and fund AOSDANA, a select body of artists who meet regularly and whose needier members are financially supported by the state.

The tradition of writers as social critics is carried on by people like Richard Kearney the philosopher, Joseph Lee the historian, Terence

Brown, Declan Kiberd and Seamus Deane the literary critics, by journalists like Fintan O'Toole, John Waters and Nuala O'Faolain, and by poets like James Simmons, John Montague, Michael Hartnett, Gerald Dawe, Seamus Heaney, Theo Dorgan, Hugh Maxton, Ann Hartigan and others. Again, the powerful presence of women poets must be noted and praised; writers such as Evan Boland, Nuala Ní Domhnaill, Elaine Ní Chuilleanain, Sara Berkeley, Rosemarie Rowley, Katie Donovan, Julie O'Callaghan, Leland Bardwell, Rita Ann Higgins, Paula Meehan, Mary O'Donnell, Áine Ní Glinn, Eithne Strong, Rosita Boland, Maeve McGuckian and others come to mind. Edna Longley, the distinguished literary critic, and the artist Constance Short work hard to stimulate and sharpen political and cultural consciousness north and south of the Border.

Below *A double image of Cork's waterside architecture. Founded on reclaimed marshland (the Irish name Corcaigh means 'marshy place'), the city today is a port, university town and cultural center keen to assert its independence from Dublin.*

There's a special force in the writings of these women. A very special, personal, resonant force. It is the kind of force that is crucial in the fight against the closed mind. This force is typical of the voices of victims who have become creators and critics. This force is evident also in the work of women writers of a previous generation, such as Mary Lavin and Kate O'Brien, who in more difficult and more oppressive times fought the good fight and wrote the good write against the closed mind.

What does one do with a closed mind? Open it up. And *everyone* (or nearly everyone!) can contribute to this opening up. Businessmen, lawyers, journalists, priests, civil servants, teachers, doctors, academics, sportsmen and sportswomen and their supporters, politicians, readers of newspapers, listeners to radio and viewers of television, *all* have their opportunity, ability and responsibility to lift the darkness from the heart and mind of Ireland. There are so many problems, situations and personalities that we must try to understand.

It is impossible to understand Ireland without thinking of England. They are physically close and politically bound up with each other, but they have never, until recently, really *spoken* to each other. They are speaking to each other now. Leading politicians from both countries are conducting a serious dialogue on "the Irish problem." Good will come of it.

England is a great country, but in its dealings with Ireland it has often been insensitive, heedless and unjust. We Irish, in our turn, have often been violent, perverse and ignorant in our dealings with England and the English. Why? That is what we must try to understand.

We must continue to speak to each other, to talk things out. To open up. It is the only way to dispel the sinister shadows thrown by the ancient antagonisms.

Even at this late stage I believe that the IRA or their representatives should be invited to speak to the Irish people on radio and television, and the Irish people be allowed to speak back. What we need is full, honest communication, not murderous bombs, not cowardly assassinations. Do not totally isolate subversives, terrorists and revolutionaries. An imposed isolation strengthens the closed mind. In isolation it will simply justify its actions to itself more and more. With dialogue there is at

Below *Lush pastures and contented cows are still part of rural Ireland, but industrial products and exports now outstrip agricultural ones and the majority of Irish people are thoroughly urban in their aspirations and lifestyle.*

least a hope of opening it up. Let the IRA speak in public to the people they are claiming to liberate, and let us discuss why and how and where this "liberation" is taking place. Then we may begin to discover who is liberating whom. We will begin to find out what is really wanted. We will see who is courageous and who is cowardly. Instead of killing each other, perhaps we can work towards a new, tolerant Ireland where every voice is heard and respected—and thought about. I am not talking about some vague political Utopia. I am talking about a small, rainy island with lovely sunny moments somewhere in the Atlantic; an island that has not yet learned to be truly tolerant; a tiny island country that is full of promise because it is fertile and beautiful and has a lot of problems and a lot of decent, hard-working intelligent people to solve these problems and go on to shape one of the most attractive countries in the world.

England is a tolerant land. Thousands upon thousands of Irishmen appreciate that fact. England saved many an Irish family from hunger and despair in the 1930s, 1940s and 1950s, but as far as Ireland is concerned, England is not a good listener.

It doesn't listen to us as it should, that is, in a spirit of goodwill and understanding. Or when it does listen, that act of compassionate listening is too brief. To the English the "Irish problem" is only one of many problems. To many Irish people the "Irish problem" is of paramount importance.

In all this a most important consideration is the matter of the Ulster Unionist. Here, too, the need for dialogue, rather than merely talking *at* each other, or not talking at all, is of prime importance. The Ulster Unionists are a strong, proud, dominant people. But they must think out their position. And they must articulate it fairly and squarely. And the IRA must talk back, fairly and squarely. And the government of the Republic must speak out in the same manner, fairly and squarely.

The continuing tragic situation in Ireland is a classic example of people refusing to speak openly to each other. Many young people, bored and appalled at the futile bombing and killing, wish to enter into an intelligent dialogue with each other.

Ireland is a country for young men and young women. They are beginning to sense their own power for good. Their minds are opening. Yet their situation is difficult. Many of them are unemployed. Unemployment is an insult to

Above *Queen's University, Belfast, founded in 1845, has a central tower modeled on that of Magdalen College, Oxford. Queen Victoria granted Belfast city status in 1888.*

Left *Girls consistently outshine boys at school and college, but are under-represented at post-graduate and research level, and in most decision-making areas of Irish life. A woman who succeeds in commerce or politics still makes headlines.*

Above *The modernization of rural Ireland has been very slow. To visitors from Britain or Europe, the countryside still appears startlingly unspoilt and unpopulated.*

human dignity. Most people want to work. Most people deeply *need* to work. Unemployment is a chronic waste of energy and talent. It is also a source of cynicism, depression and despair.

There is a lot of unemployment in Ireland now. There is more crime than ever before. A lot of crime is committed out of boredom. Boredom is generated by unemployment. Unemployment leads to crime. It is very wrong of a government to allow unemployment to rise at the rate it is rising in Ireland at present.

Yet, in spite of that, many young Irish people are thinking and talking in a fluent, creative way about their country. They see that patriotism need not, should not involve assassination and murder. They see that work and the dignity that goes with working are vital to a true, practical and visionary patriotism. The best patriot is the best worker. And many young people in Ireland are simply ravenous for work. Attention must be paid to this fact. If attention is paid, crime will diminish. Peace will be possible.

Most important of all, however, in the battle

against the closed mind is the need for education. Traditionally the Irish are great lovers of education. They have gone in search of it all over Europe. Today, however, education is largely in the hands of the middle classes, whereas it should be available to everyone. Education is still a matter of money, whereas it should be a matter of talent, of intelligence and of desire.

We must open all our universities to all our people. Money should not be necessary to get into a university. There is only one necessary qualification: ability. If a boy or a girl has the ability, he or she should be given the opportunity. This is only just. But Irish politicians lack the imagination to see this simple fact. Or if they see it, they lack the heart to implement it. And yet, already, in spite of crippled, ambitious politicians, there are great advances in education, particularly among older people.

Education is about the discovery and the development of one's nature, character and personality. It concerns the bringing out into the light of day all these talents which are buried in us. Some people do not sense these buried talents until they are well advanced in years. A good educational system will enable people to discover and develop these hidden talents. And people should be able to do this at any point in their lives.

Education should not be confined to the young. It should be available to people at their moment of need, at whatever moment in their lives they feel they need it. This may happen at 16 or at 60.

I teach in a university. Some of the best students I have seen were people older than myself. In their studies, they taught me. Education is about eternal learning. We teach each other all the time. That is true teaching, true learning.

Adult education is strong in Ireland now. People who have raised families are going back to school. And in doing so they are not only stimulating themselves; they are enlightening youngsters who are younger than their own children.

This notion that education is not confined to the young, that it does not exist simply so that one can get a job, is vital. Neither is education a luxury or a rich privilege. Education is normal, difficult, enjoyable, civilized. People have a right to it.

There is a drift towards this kind of thinking in contemporary Ireland.

One day, any intelligent Irish boy or girl, man or woman, will be able to walk into any one of our universities and say: "I wish to study Irish or English or French or Medicine or Engineering."

That day is not too far away. But we must work to bring that day closer. It is a day of justice. In modern Ireland some of the people who have worked hardest for justice are women. If I single out Nell McCafferty it is only because she has shown more aggressive energy than most others. Nell is a born writer and her campaign on behalf of women is really a campaign on behalf of justice. She is a model for Irish girls. She has her own voice, she is her own woman. She is hard-working, independent, fiery, true to her own vision. She'll put all the old stifling Irish Mothers (Mother Ireland, Mother Church, Mother Machree) where they belong. Nowhere. Nell is in the tradition of Countess Markievicz, Lady Gregory, Maud Gonne, Bernadette Devlin and Sister Stanislaus Kennedy.

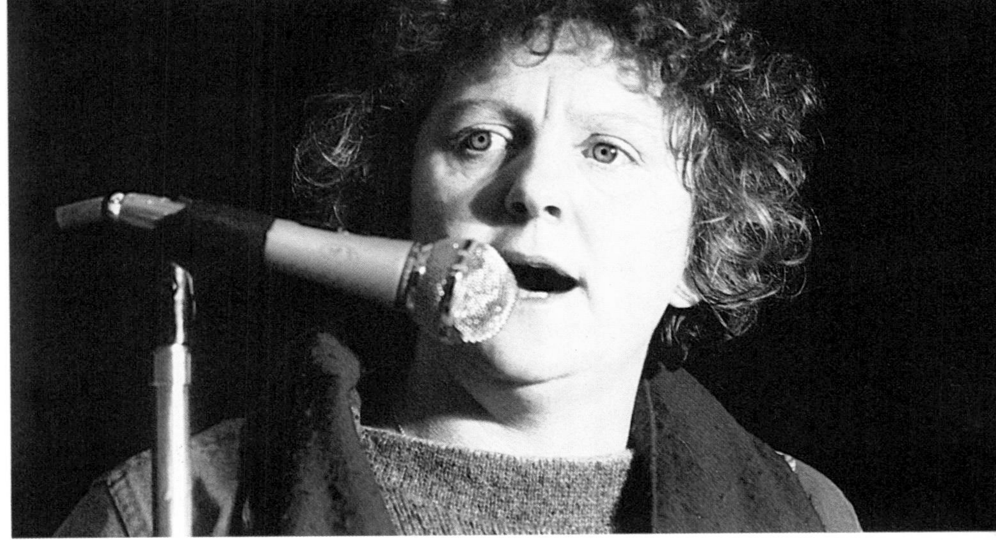

Above *Journalist and feminist Nell McCafferty is a witty, outspoken and compassionate participant in Ireland's struggle toward a new order.*

The new, young and extremely effective President of Ireland is a woman, Mary Robinson. Her election had behind it the passionate dreams and articulate support of hundreds of thousands of women, young and old. She is

doing an excellent job in an elegant, strong and eloquent way. She symbolizes a new kind of hope for the country.

Miraculously, Ireland has always produced such women. They are strong when others are weak, valorous when others are cowardly and subservient. Nell McCafferty's writings about law and justice are among the most important social documents to come out of Ireland during the last half-century and more. Women are now deeply concerned with law and justice. Why wouldn't they be? For too long they were victims. Now they are active thinkers.

This new, active, thinking, articulate Irishwoman may help even a lot of Irishmen to grow up!

It would be foolish to confuse the process of getting older with the process of growing up. The Catholic Church is two thousand years old but it still refuses women the right to become priests. The Catholic Church is therefore rejecting one of its most valuable sources of spiritual energy and passion. Throughout its history Ireland has always owed a really profound debt to its women. A church which refuses women the right to become priests is simply being perverse, not recognizing its own potential, cutting its own throat, determined to remain stuck in a predictable spiritual rut. Two thousand years old. Refusing to grow up.

Growing up can be a painful process. Sean O'Casey said that "Ireland is the oldest civilisation in Europe but she is still in her teens." A teenage island, old as the sea it squats in. Opening its eyes. Stretching forth its hands. Growing up.

Sometimes I think Ireland is growing up against its own will, that it prefers to destroy itself, its fine people. Why can't *all* the terrorists see that they are not helping Ireland to grow up? Or are they committed to the non-growing of this country? Are they determined to maim and cripple all good growth? Is terrorism terrified of the potential in ordinary, decent living? Does it hate the promise in normality?

If patriotism means anything nowadays, surely it is a kind of communal charity, a willingness to work and grow together, a sort of casual helping each other, a fluently co-operative attitude, something normal and con-

Left *An otherworldly sunset at Recess in Connemara, County Galway.*

sistent and good-willed and day-to-day.

In Ireland we have to learn more and more to help each other in this way. Catholic and Protestant and Jew, agnostic and atheist, Unionist and Nationalist, city people and country people, Church and State—all must work together to produce the new Ireland, the Ireland that will emerge from trouble and darkness, from ignorance and prejudice, from tragedy and suspicion and self-destruction and intolerance. We have begun our journey into tolerance and understanding. We still have a long way to go.

Tolerance is a pleasant and blessed land; the journey towards it is arduous and self-challenging. That is the journey Ireland has to make.

Instead of killing, we must create. Instead of hating, we must love. Instead of sneering, we must encourage. This may seem a romantic

Below *Faces in the crowd, Dublin Carnival.*

dream. It is not. It is a real possibility. To achieve it, we must get rid of the closed mind for good and glory. We must open up to each other, especially to what we sense is most different and difficult in each other. If we do this we will discover the Ireland in our hearts, the Ireland that has survived all kinds of violence, including violent parodies of itself; not a sentimental Ireland, not a place to sing sloppy ballads or tell mawkish yarns about, not a cynical, derisive and divisive island, but a keen, intelligent, beautiful and humorous country with people who, knowing each other's creeds, beliefs and politics, are prepared, in the thoughtful decency of their hearts and minds, to tolerate each other, to enjoy each other.

That's not Utopia.

That's Ireland.

Index

Page numbers in italics refer to illustrations and captions

Bibliography

Bradley, Anthony, *William Butler Yeats*, 1979, The Frederick Unger Publishing Co.

Bolger, Dermot (Ed.), *Letters from the New Ireland*, 1991, Raven Arts Press.

Brown, Terence, *Ireland: A Social and Cultural History*, 1981, Fontana.

Clarke, Austin, *Flight to Africa*, 1963, Dolmen Press.

de Breffny, Brian (Ed.), *Ireland: A Cultural Encyclopedia*, 1983, Thames & Hudson.

Facts about Ireland, 1985, Department of Foreign Affairs.

Foster, R. F., *Modern Ireland, (1600–1972)*, 1988, Penguin Books.

Foster, R. F. (Ed.), *The Oxford Illustrated History of Ireland*, 1989, Oxford University Press.

Gmelch, Sharon (Ed.), *Irish Life*, 1979, O'Brien Press.

Gwynn, Stephen, *Reminiscences of a Literary Man*, 1976, Thomas Nelson & Sons Ltd.

Jeffares, A. N. (Ed.), *Yeats's Poems*, 1989, Papermac Macmillan.

Joyce, James, *Ulysses*, 1952, Bodley Head.

Kee, Robert, *Ireland: A History*, 1980, Weidenfeld & Nicolson.

Kennedy, Kieran A., Giblin, Thomas and McHugh, Deirdre, *The Economic Development of Ireland in the Twentieth Century*, 1988, Routledge.

Kennelly, Brendan, *Moloney Up And At It*, 1984, Mercier Press.

Keynes, Geoffrey (Ed.), *The Poetry and Prose of William Blake*, 1961, Nonesuch Library.

Lawlor, H. J. (Trans.). *St Bernard of Clairvaux: Life of St Malachy of Armagh*, 1920, London.

Lee, J. J., *Ireland 1945–85*, 1989, Cambridge University Press.

Litton, Frank (Ed.), *Unequal Achievement: The Irish Experience 1957–1982*, 1982, The Institute of Public Administration.

Love is for Life, 1985, The Irish Bishops' Pastoral.

Lydon, J. F., *Ireland and England in the Latter Middle Ages*, 1981, Irish Academic Press.

Lydon, J. F., *The Lordship of Ireland in the Middle Ages*, 1972, Gill & Macmillan.

Lyons, F. S. L., *Culture and Anarchy in Ireland*, 1982, Oxford Univeristy Press.

Lyons, F. S. L., *Ireland Since the Famine*, 1971, Weidenfeld & Nicolson.

MacCurtain, Margaret and O'Dowd, Mary (Eds.), *Women in Early Modern Ireland*, 1991, Wolfhound Press.

MacManus, Francis, *The Years of the Great Test 1929–39*, 1967, Mercier Press.

MacNiaocaill, Gearóld, *Ireland Before the Vikings*, 1972, Gill & Macmillan.

Moody, T. W. and Martin, F. X. (Eds.), *The Course of Irish History*, 1967, Mercier Press.

Mould, Daphne Pochin, *The Aran Islands*, 1977, David & Charles.

Murphy, John A., *Ireland in the 20th Century*, 1975, Gill & Macmillan.

O'Connor, Frank, *The Backward Look*, 1967, London.

O'Toole, Fintan, *A Mass for Jessie James: A Journey through 1980s Ireland*, 1990, Raven Arts Press.

O'Tuathaigh, Gearoid, *Ireland Before the Famine*, 1990, Gill & Macmillan.

Otway-Ruthven, A. J., *A History of Mediaeval Ireland*, 1967, London.

Synge, John, *Collected Plays*, 1982, Colin Smythe.

Waters, John, *Jiving at the Crossroads*, 1991, Blackstaff.

Webb, G. C. (Ed.), *Metalogicon*, 1929, Oxford.

Picture Credits

Aerofilms 22 **Andrew Lawson** 37, 152-153, 168 **BBC Hulton Picture Library** 58, 71 top, 81, 82, 85 bottom **Central Press Photos** 158 left **Bill Doyle** 16-17, 106, 116, 125, 126, 127, 129 right, 132-133, 134-135, 138, 140-141, 176, 178-179, 182 **British Library** 45 **Dublin Office of Public Works** 31 right, 42, 46, 47, 47 right, 52 **G. A. Duncan** 84 bottom, 89 left, 172 left **E. T. Archive** 62 **Mark Fiennes** 10, 69, 83 left and right, 87 top, 88, 90, 93 right, 103 top, 113 right, 115, 133 right **Inpho-Allsport** 153 right **Inpho Sports Photography** Alan Betson 158, 160, 175 right James Meehan 102 bottom, 148 left, 148-149, 162-163 Billy Stickland front cover (bottom right), 130, 139, 143, 144, 145, 147, 149 right,151, 154-155, 156-157, 159, 164-165 **Irish Tourist Board** endpapers, half title page, 7, 14-15, 21 right, 32, 34, 35, 36, 39, 40, 41 left and right, 43 left and right, 44 top, 46 left, 49, 50, 59 left, 64-65, 66 left, 68, 70, 71 right, 72, 84 top, 89 right, 94-95, 129 left, 156 left, 161, 166, 169 **Tom Kelly** 12 left, 18, 75 top right, 135 right, 172-173 **Mansell Collection** 76-77, 77 right **National Gallery of Ireland** 44 bottom, 60-61, 74-75, 85 top **National Irish Tourist Board** 181 **National Library of Ireland** 78-79 **National Museum of Ireland** 15 right, 23, 26 **National Portrait Gallery** 63 bottom, 173 right **National Trust** 63 top **Newnes Books** 27, 28, 38 **Northern Ireland Tourist Board** 51, 67 right **Pacemaker Press** 96 left **Pictures for Print** front cover (top), title page, 75 bottom right, 86, 100, 110, 170-171, 178 left **Pieterse-Davison International** 79 right **Press Association International Limited** 80 **Rex Features** 97 **The Slide File** 20, 24-25, 29, 30, 31 left, 48, 53 bottom, 57, 61 right, 91, 98, 109, 111, 117, 118-119, 120-121, 124, 128, 131, 136-137, 150 **Spectrum** 6, 12-13, 56, 66-67, 73, 99 bottom, 100-101, 107, 174-175, 177 **Derek Speirs** contents spread, 87 bottom, 96 right, 99 top, 108, 112 left, 114, 183 **Derek Speirs/Report** 140 left, 142 **Tony Stone Associates** 92-93 **Don Sutton** front cover (2nd from top and bottom left), back cover, 54-55, 59 right, 102 top, 122-123, 184-185, 186-187 **ZEFA Picture Library** 8-9, 33, 53 top, 95 right, 104-105, 112-113

Multimedia Books have endeavored to observe the legal requirements with regard to suppliers of photographic material.